Buy Here Pay Here
Real Estate

Master the Art of Money Making Money

Larry L. Bieda

Buy Here Pay Here Real Estate:
Master the Art of Money Making Money

Copyright © 2011 by Larry L. Bieda

ISBN: 1467920096
ISBN-13: 978-1467920094

First Printing, December 2011

www.LarryBieda.com

Praise for *Buy Here Pay Here Real Estate*

"Larry Bieda will be the next generation's Mark Zuckerberg for real estate. After all, it's innovation, ingenuity and creativity that's rewarded in business today. This book highlights his revolutionary 'sign and reside' approach that makes housing accessible to all."

—**Frank McKinney,** Real Estate "Artist" and five-time bestselling author, including *Burst This! Frank McKinney's Bubble-Proof Real Estate Strategies,* www.Burst-This.com

"Larry Bieda is a visionary real estate leader with real, practical ideas that can help real estate investors. Put into practice, Larry's 'Buy Here Pay Here' concept has the potential to have a tremendous positive impact on the housing market."

—**Uri Man,** Global Market Strategist, FOX Business

"Larry offers an easy read that shows you how to achieve financial success through real estate no matter where you are today financially or what you do for a living. His 'think-out-of-the-box' method is well worth studying because, regardless of your financial situation, you can benefit from his advice."

—**M. Gary Neuman,** *New York Times* bestselling author, practicing licensed counselor and ordained rabbi who has also appeared on *Today, The View,* NPR and many other programs. Oprah has referred to him as, "One of the best psychotherapists in the world."

*For the Buyers, Lenders and Investors
who make the American Dream possible*

CONTENTS

AUTHOR'S INTRODUCTION

Buy Here Pay Here Real Estate® is a revolutionary concept that not only applies to real estate, but also serves as an ideal business model designed to show you how to navigate in today's challenging and confusing financial arena. This unique approach to real estate, my life's work so far, has proven itself over and over again to work for more than a decade. I am excited to present it to you in this book and share with you my multifaceted approach to financial success.

I will show you how utilizing Buy Here Pay Here Real Estate strategies made me a teenage millionaire and now has placed me solidly in that notorious "One Percent," while I'm still a twenty-something. Although I do sympathize with the utter frustration and disillusionment underlying the "Occupy Wall Street" protest movement, which is occurring as I write this Introduction, you will see that I offer a viable and proven solution: Buy Here Pay Here Real Estate. If you occupy the ideas set forth in this book, it can change your outlook and make you wealthy, too.

Typically, when analyzing deals most people look for the highest ROI, which we've all been taught means

"Return On Investment." Yet in this troubling financial climate, it is quickly becoming apparent that this typical approach, along with much of the status quo and old ways of doing business, has become extinct. Buy Here Pay Here Real Estate offers you something that no other system does: the modernization and radical transformation of outdated modes of thinking. It takes the stodgy old ROI principle and transforms it into a totally new concept:

ROI = "Retire On Interest!"

Unlike other systems focused on regurgitating their own (or even others') specific techniques, Buy Here Pay Here Real Estate puts you in the driver's seat on the road to financial riches equipped with a wealth of proven methods to navigate any financial terrain. Here you'll be encouraged to think out-of-the-box and draw outside the lines. It is all about creating the deal, not just buying it, and learning how to be a deal maker...not a deal breaker. It is that innovative approach that will give you the edge over the competition. I know it works—I have personally done it countless times and continue to do so today. My system is your GPS to an exciting future and provides you the only tools and road map you'll need with easy-to-follow directions.

Many people find themselves disenchanted and join movements such as "Occupy Wall Street." But remember, the ultimate stimulus program is within each of us. You can live a rewarding, stimulating and enriching life by *"Occupying Real Estate"!* I am passionate about sharing my secrets with you and teaching you how to think creatively to attain your dreams of financial riches. The options are endless and are only limited to your imagination!

Warmest wishes for your financial
enlightenment and success,

Larry L. Bieda

CHAPTER 1

WILL YOU BE RICH OR POOR? THE CHOICE IS YOURS!

During a recent flight between Ixtapa, Mexico, and Houston, Texas, sitting in an oversized leather first-class seat with the smell of freshly warmed almonds permeating the air and lace curtains imparting a separation between the classes, I realized that the plane symbolized the composition of the world's socio-economic classes and the future of America's class system: one without a middle class—just first class and coach.

First class provides the best of everything: free-flowing wine, delicious gourmet meals, hot towels, cheerful personalized service, and a private bathroom with fresh gardenias reserved for the elite few. On the other hand, coach offers only the bare necessities: no free wine, no free meal, no towels, and unpleasant bathrooms shared by the masses. Inspired by the opulence of first class, I began putting pen to paper and started writing this book about Buy Here Pay Here Real Estate, a revolutionary system where people from all walks of life can partake in its bounty.

In Mexico, I found the private beach hammock a great place to reward myself for all of my hard work, giving me a much-needed opportunity to recharge my batteries. But along the way I discovered that the journey to that restful destination was even better. You see, life itself is a journey and although money is not everything, it sure makes the experience more enjoyable!

It is my belief that everyone makes a choice whether to be rich or poor. You may be reading this book because you have arrived at that fork in the road, or you may just be tired of losing money in the stock market or losing control of your investments while following the same old strategies.

As I write this book, thousands of young people are taking part in a protest called "Occupy Wall Street." I traveled to New York to meet with them directly and hear what many of them had to say. While I sympathize with their frustration, I explained to them, as I also want to show you, that it is within your power to change your life.

Members of today's dwindling middle class find themselves groping for guaranteed pensions and much relied upon retirement benefits. The lucky few who remain may only have a 401(k) to depend on before being sent on their way.

The prosperity of the good life is entirely up to you, which can be both exciting as well as intimidating if you don't know what you are doing. But it is never too late (or too early) to learn. And this is where the Buy Here Pay Here Real Estate System comes in. It is a groundbreaking business method that gives you a blueprint for your road to financial riches.

As a self-taught entrepreneur, self-made millionaire, financial prodigy, author and real estate deal expert, I bought my first foreclosure at age 17, and made my first million by age 19. I've written this book to share with you my unique experiences and to educate you in a way that few books do: teaching investment strategies and investment intelligence based on the wealth of my *actual experiences* in the world, not something I learned in a classroom. You cannot learn from a book what you can learn from actual experience. I encourage you to use my insight to open up new doors for you to succeed beyond your wildest dreams!

People often ask me, what is a financial prodigy? My answer is: somebody who has never repressed his or her passion for money. Our society tends to judge people who are ardent about growing their wealth as greedy, materialistic, manipulative as Wall Street, and even un-spiritual. But a financial prodigy realizes from a young age that none of these are the case.

Now I attended kindergarten and grade school just like almost everyone else. Yet how many people do you know who, as five-year-olds, converted their balcony into a condo and went over carpet samples with their sister, trying to sell her a unit? The fire in my belly for making money has always been there. It never got extinguished. In fact, anybody's skeptical opinions or judgments only fueled my creative development of strategies and systems that prove:

There is a teachable art to how money makes money, and it's an art that anyone can learn.

When I purchased my first home at age 17, I spent every available moment outside of school renovating the property. Within a matter of months, I sold the property for a hefty $117,000 profit. I took some of the profit and invested it into another property, making yet another $80,000. As prices in the city started to soar, I took those profits and started investing in rural towns, undaunted by challenges that included working with local municipalities, zoning consultants, architects and engineers. Before long, I was building homes, up-zoning properties, and virtually changing the landscape of towns. The community response taught me the importance of giving back, and today, as a philanthropist, one of my greatest unexpected joys is building quality affordable housing (you will learn my definition of what that is later in this book). In fact, this has become a hallmark of much of my work.

Although a few obvious clues in my youth pointed to my passion for real estate, I could not have predicted my path, nor did I try. I didn't think about growing rich. I just followed my instincts and never denied or apologized for my passion for money.

While in grade school, I began reading every book that I could get my hands on that had to do with the subject of money and investing. Many of these books are available through the store on my blog at www.LarryBieda.com. In my opinion, they all a must-read if you are serious about your financial future.

**The choice is yours: First-class or coach?
Rich or poor?**

Learning how to make money and save it is no longer enough.

It is what you do with it that will buy you into a first-class lifestyle and all of the privileges that go with it. Don't just give your hard-earned money over to your stockbroker.

As I settled into my richly appointed leather seat, I looked around the first-class cabin, observing the many different types of people. I think the guy sitting next to me may be your stockbroker and he is occupying what should be your seat...LOL!

Reclaim your first-class seat by taking control of your money. If you are smart enough to earn it and save it, why haven't you taken the initiative to control and invest it yet?!

As I am about to teach you in this book, Buy Here Pay Here Real Estate holds a solution for you, one so simple and obvious, it's gone under the radar until now.

Before we delve any further, let's first take care of some housekeeping. For the purpose of brevity and clarity, a brief explanation of terms follows below. They may be used interchangeably.

Buy Here Pay Here Real Estate may be shortened to BHPH Real Estate. Master it and the world is your oyster. Learn it and earn yourself a BHPH degree in real estate wealth creation, management and preservation.

Buyers are also termed end-users (or owner occupants). Ultimately, the buyer is the one whom the investor/lender markets the property to. Investors may also be sellers, flippers, or landlords. Lenders can be a bank, a hard-money lender, a partner in a joint venture, or any combination of these.

All of these terms are further detailed in "The Vision" in Chapter 7.

Creative mixing and matching is the name of the game. It is the art of putting lenders, buyers and investors productively and synergistically together, not just buyers and sellers together. Whether you are a lender, buyer, or investor, the BHPH Real Estate approach has the investments, strategies and system in place that can launch you on your way to buying your ticket to financial freedom and continued success.

In light of today's unprecedented financial crisis, we can no longer count on conventional financing. So we need to focus on creative financing...and that is exactly what BHPH does in real estate.

Throughout the last several years, real estate values have experienced one of the greatest disappearing acts in history. I can't help but wonder, where have all the buyers gone and where did all the lenders go?

I have a unique advantage of having seen real estate at its historic highs as well as its lows. It did not make sense that when prices were so high everyone wanted to jump on the bandwagon and buy, but now when prices are so low, buyers are occupying the sidelines. You play the contrarian and get into the game. I'll coach. You score.

During the heyday, lenders were giving out huge loans to practically anyone with a pulse. But now that their coffers have been padded with government bailouts (meaning your money as well as mine), loans are practically non-existent. It is often said that the rich get richer and the poor get poorer, but in actuality it has a lot to do with our spending and buying habits. For instance, when there is a sale, the rich buy out the assets. Whereas the poor wait for sales on cell phones, computers and televisions that will never go up in value.

Because I work in real estate, many people ask me how I am different from the multitude of multimillionaire entrepreneurs that invest in real estate. I am just a regular guy, but my rags-to-riches story distinctively sets my work and the BHPH Real Estate approach apart. Most importantly, rather than focus on real estate investments unrelated to your life's work as a means to growing rich, I teach people that it really doesn't matter what your work is, so long as you are selling products or providing services you are passionate about in order to yield a lasting fortune. I also teach that real estate investments can work—but they don't have to be high-end luxury ones that fulfill the desires of a select few. There is, in fact, a way to serve an under served and growing population in need of affordable homes. And by strategically investing in their American Dream, we can exponentially realize ours, while continuing to do exactly the work we love and were born to do.

Because I've been able to accumulate great wealth and live my ideal lifestyle this way, my mission now is to create a society of people who live their dreams because they know how to cultivate financial wealth by implementing strategies found in BHPH Real Estate that no other business method will teach you. My goal is to foster a culture of investing...not passive investing, but what I call *"intimate investing"* through which you can reap financial rewards from all of the opportunities out there.

I recognized in my early teens that our educational system does not teach financial intelligence, so I embarked on a journey seeking out successful people to mentor me. Today, I take this renegade approach one step further by offering what I learned on my odyssey and putting it into the easy-to-learn, step-by-step methods found in this book.

Perhaps you haven't yet pursued a higher education or your passion is to voice your frustration and Occupy Wall Street. Or maybe you've earned a college degree but your bank balance makes you wonder whether it was worth it as you're deep in debt with student loans. Or perhaps you are just looking to take more control over the money that you do have. Well, it may surprise you to know that you are in good company. Some of the richest and most successful people in the world made their fortune without graduating from college. Some of them went for a few semesters at most, while others dropped out of high school. A few examples of these are:

- **Michael Dell**, founder and CEO of Dell, Inc., dropped out of college at age 19. He first started his computer company in his college dorm room. Today his estimated net worth is $12.3 billion.

- **Henry Ford** never graduated high school, yet he went on to start one of the largest automobile manufacturing companies in the world, Ford Motor Company. He has been called one of the most influential people of the twentieth century.

- **Bill Gates,** founder of Microsoft, is a college dropout. He has been named one of the richest people in the world with a net worth of over $40 billion.

- **Steve Jobs,** the late co-founder and former CEO of Apple, dropped out of college and went on to pioneer the personal computer era. His signature "Think Different" campaign revolutionized communications, brought him billions, and made us all his iGroupies.

- **Steven Spielberg** is a movie producer and director. He was denied acceptance to film school and dropped out of California State University. He co-founded DreamWorks, a major film studio that has produced some of the highest-gross ing movie hits in history. He has an estimated net worth of $3 billion.

- **Mark Zuckerberg,** the founder of Facebook, dropped out of Harvard. Today his estimated net worth is in excess of $15 billion.

Then there is myself, Larry Bieda. I left college after a few weeks, realizing that my fortunes were not going to be made sitting in a classroom, but by going out into the world where I could put my experience, knowledge and vision to work. Over the years, I have applied my BHPH formula to real estate, which enabled me to transact over 1,000 properties representing many millions of dollars of real estate. Along the way, I developed my philosophy that everyone deserves to achieve the American Dream and enjoy pride of ownership. BHPH Real Estate offers buyers and investors creative programs that feature a convenient one-stop shopping approach where every aspect of the home buying and investment experience is covered. I am proud to have an education based on real-world experience where my astute observations and in-sights make me uniquely qualified as an expert on how to achieve financial success.

And this list barely touches the surface of the successful people who went on to make millions and billions of dollars without going to college. The web site CollegeDropoutHallofFame.com is a great place to check out other people who became successful without graduating college, or even high school.

In any case, I've written this book for you, no matter what your situation may be.

I invite you to occupy my mind for a while as you might find it to be a stimulating place to stake out.

After leaving college, I found that there were few books to pick up and reference the success of people who did not attend higher education. What's more, not even the best-selling financial books of our time had the gumption to be forthright and tell it like it is: higher education is in the business of taking your money, not making you money. If I were to establish an institution, take money and give out pieces of paper (a.k.a. diplomas and degrees) and not guarantee you could get a job with that piece of paper, it would be considered fraud. But colleges and universities legally do this, while students borrow and take full-recourse loans not dischargeable by bankruptcy. All of this usually occurs when their students are between the impressionable ages of 18 and 22, not knowing their rear ends from their heads.

All things considered, this book is the one I would have wanted to be available to me. Its intention is to teach you what I have been teaching private clients for years. I firmly believe—and it is the same reason that I am in affordable housing—that if you want to become rich, you have to do more things for more people for less money. This book is a case in point, because with it I am able to help people by spreading financial enlightenment to the masses and planting the seed in people's minds that going to school and being average is *not* the only way. Instead of being ordinary, you can be extraordinary! And you can live your dream while helping others achieve theirs.

Henry Ford's goal was to democratize the automobile. Mine is to democratize real estate by what I envision as real estate "dealerships," and by extension the way money makes money. A real estate office should be like a car dealership where you walk in, sign some papers and drive out with the vehicle of your dreams. Real estate dreams should be just as easy to realize. And they can be. Believe me. I know from personal experience.

The current system is broken. There are not enough jobs for the numbers of people receiving training. If you do not fit into one mold, the system attempts to pound you into another while distracting you from learning, if not outright withholding the facts, about how to master the art of money making money. Only business majors receive any kind of training in entrepreneurship and investing. Yet given the number of unemployed MBAs hunting for work, how effective can it really be?

The truth is that you do not have to settle for the status quo. No matter what, real estate investing is for you on some level, and my business system will help you find where you fit in best. Whether you are an established professional with money in savings, stocks, bonds, mutual funds or somewhere else, a college graduate in debt with student loans up to your eyeballs, or a recent graduate lacking the clarity of what to do next (or whatever your situation may be), you can realize your financial potential and create the luxurious lifestyle that you have always dreamed of while watching others achieve it. This book reveals many tools I have designed to help you first understand where you are now monetarily and then determine where you want to and can be!

What sets this book apart from other bestselling self-help and financial titles is that it teaches you the most important thing: *how to get there.*

Read this book carefully. Its pages and their supplemental resources will reveal the precise, easy-to-follow steps you need to take in order to reach your loftiest financial goals. You will quickly grasp why all this information is required reading.

In this book, I redefine everything that you thought you knew about real estate and investments in a powerful, new way that will revolutionize your approach to it and ultimately help you achieve your financial success.

So keep reading. Your journey is just beginning. Enjoy immersing yourself in the art and business of money making money!

CHAPTER 2

MY OWN STORY—AND WHY I WANT YOU TO BE RICH, TOO

My life started out simply. In March of 1985, I was born to a loving mother, the middle child between my older sister and younger brother. As ordinary as this entrée into life may seem, no two lives ever follow the same path. Based on the unique events and stressors (yes, especially those!) in our lives, we all turn out special and different in our own ways.

My parents got divorced when I was eight years old. After my father left us high and dry, my mother had to work two and three jobs to provide for us. Times were tough. I am sure you have experienced your own challenges and can relate on some level. Yet we always pulled together, which strengthened us and enabled us to carve out extraordinary experiences from whatever came our way.

I remember the first time we were able to save money. I began selling pizza by the slice and French fries to kids after school. You see, an eight-slice pie was $10 (not 9-9-9 as one presidential aspirant espoused!) and included delivery. I sold each slice for $2 so I netted $6 per pie. I made even more money on the French fries! It was the first of many successful business ventures. I learned quickly that it did not take a lot of money or skills to start a business. After all, what skills did I have at that age? I did not know how to make a pizza or French fries; I did not have any equipment or storefront; and for that matter, I wasn't even old enough to drive. All I did was take $10 and make $6 profit: 60%...not bad for a kid! This exemplifies on a small scale the art of money making money. The more pies I bought, the more I made, and there was never any waste. If there were any leftovers, I ate them! I grew fast... in both age and size!

You see, by adding value to an already existing item, even a kid can beat the bank's return, and Wall Street's return for that matter. And this works on a much larger scale; after all, it is done every day. Look at Wal-Mart. What do they make? What about 7-11? Most of what these companies sell, they flip. They buy low and sell high.

Cardinal rule: Buy it for one price, mark it up, and sell it for another price.

Why can't you go to a big-box wholesaler like Costco and buy a soda for 30 cents instead of $1 at 7-11 for instance? Sure you can, but the store adds value that is not visible to the naked eye: *convenience.* Just like I ordered the pizza and had it conveniently there when the kids wanted it after school, it is the same way with 7-11: they have cold sodas on display right when you walk in the door, and you can be out of there in minutes. In my life, I discovered that I can apply these money-making methods to another necessary and highly lucrative asset class known as real estate. In fact, how to add convenience is one of many "value-add" techniques taught in the BHPH Real Estate System. So early on, I decided that if I were going to occupy something, it might as well be something lucrative like real estate.

More wealth has been created through real estate than any other investment in the world. However, today you need to add value to your investments beyond a few cosmetic repairs.

Kitchens, baths and what is known as "curb appeal" are no longer the only thing that sells homes. A home with a solid-gold toilet may not sell for any more than a home with a porcelain toilet. In this book, you will learn innovative value-add strategies that effectively sell homes — in any economy.

So eventually, through my pizza-flipping business combined with my other businesses such as baby-sitting services and tutoring, my family was able to save over $700. At that time, that was a ton of money for us. We kept it hidden in a thermos and added to it as often as we could. I would wish that I had more time to focus on earning more so I could save even more money. But being only 10 at the time, I was still in school.

Over the next few years, I had a variety of business ideas that enabled me to apply many of the techniques I learned to the different businesses and products on a small scale. The more I went to school, the more I realized that there was something missing. School provided only a limited and generic education. Most of my teachers themselves were struggling financially. When I saw the cars they drove and the areas they lived in, I couldn't help but wonder: if they are so smart, why aren't they rich? I concluded that the knowledge they teach is not the only knowledge necessary to be a financial success. It quickly became apparent to me that you could be a scholastic success but not necessarily a financial one.

At a young age I heard the saying "you are who you hang out with," so I decided to hang out with rich, successful people. I was not sure the best way to go about this at first. When I was a pre-teen, I devised a plan to get to know some of the wealthiest people that I could get access to and pick their brains. I realized that many of my friends' parents fell into this category. So I decided to get myself invited over for a "play date" and once I was in their homes, I would spend most of the time in the kitchen talking with the parents while the kids were upstairs playing video games.

With this strategy, I was able to learn a lot from people in a variety of businesses. Some of my friends' parents were doctors, lawyers, or accountants who were extremely smart. The others owned businesses. But my favorite of all of them were the real estate investors. Their work really appealed to me because they seemed like they were virtually able to print money by applying the same cardinal rule I had already mastered in other areas: buying a property for one price, marking it up, and selling it for a higher price.

The simplicity of it was inspiring! Across the board, they all gave me the same advice: study hard, get good grades, and do what you love. Be true to who you are and the money will follow. Some also would mention books for me to read and I jumped at the chance to get them. Again, those must-read books can also be found at www.LarryBieda.com. They truly helped shape who I am today and they can motivate you, too.

I continued to pick people's brains well into my teen years, which enabled me to amass a lot of knowledge. Many of these people became my mentors, and I remain in touch with many of them. That mentorship, combined with the books I read, gave me a clear view of how I wanted to make money once I graduated.

On one occasion, I met with a very successful local builder and asked if I could shadow him for a few days and learn about how he conducts business. He not only welcomed the suggestion, but went so far as to have me spend several days working alongside his project manager. He also gave me his coveted contact information for several of his vendors and even lenders. I was amazed at his openness and asked him why he was being so forthright and nice to me. His answer remains with me to this day.

He explained that when he first started out, someone showed him the ropes and gave him all the know-how he would need to succeed in business with one caveat: one day he would need to repay the favor by teaching someone else what he learned. Essentially, to "pay it forward." And one of my goals is to do my part by continuing the legacy of paying it forward to the next generation through the insights I am able to share with you in this book. You, dear reader, are my payback.

After years of living in rental housing and hearing about the importance of owning your own home, I decided to take on the mission of getting me and my family out of the rental market and realizing the American Dream for ourselves. I discussed the idea of home ownership with my mother and she was on board. So together we began our search.

At age 16, I got my driver's license as soon as possible because I knew that having my own transportation would mean having my freedom. I was able to go look at deals, go to the library, and network with people. I spent many days and countless hours driving through different neighborhoods comparing houses and prices. It was very scary to cold-call realtors, especially when you don't know what you are talking about. But I knew it was a good way to cut my teeth.

By age 17, I found _the_ deal.

It was a three-bedroom, two-bathroom home, with a pool, located in a great neighborhood. It was a foreclosure and needed everything! We had our work cut out for us. My mother hesitated at first, wondering how we would do all of the work. I assured her that if we bought the house, I would learn everything it takes to get the house fixed up. She expressed concern about where we would get the money. I explained what I had learned: _if the deal were good enough, the money would follow._

And it did. We did not take no for an answer: we

went door-to-door and peer-to-peer and no lender or investor was too big or too small for us to approach. After all, we were, and still are, *equal opportunity borrowers!*

Once we closed on the house, I rolled up my sleeves and went to work. I remember one night my mother pulled in after a long night of work. She found me working in the front yard, with construction lights on, painting the outside of the house. It was very late and dark outside and I was trying to distinguish which color paint was for the trim and which for the walls. I often went to school with paint under my fingernails and drywall dust around my nose, possibly in my lungs, but definitely in my heart. It must have looked like I was on cocaine! Maybe I was a little bit high from the paint fumes, but I loved it and learned a lot. I knew I would not be painting and plastering forever, but I understood that in order to hire people to do these jobs, I would need to know how to do it as well so that I would know what a good job should look like.

When the home was finished, it was time to sell. Our downside was if the house did not sell, we had a beautiful place to live, or we could rent it out for income. Our upside was that we would walk away with a ton of money. The home quickly sold at the highest price, dollar per square foot in that neighborhood's history at that time! We gladly accepted the offer. The closing took place two weeks into my entering university.

So I did what any other brilliant, motivated college student would do…I dropped out to start my own real estate investment company.

With the confidence of that first deal under my belt, I went out and repeated the process. *Buy-fix-flip; wash-rinse-repeat.* I bought the home six doors down and repeated the system by flipping that one as well...been there, flipped that...and so on!

We began attending real estate auctions and developed a lot of contacts with realtors, brokers, and asset managers who specialized in foreclosures and distressed properties. Our territory began to grow. And the market began to rise.

One day, there were two auctions scheduled at the same time, so I decided to go to the one in the northern part of the city, while my mother went to bid on the one in the southern part of the city. Well into the auction, I received a phone call from her explaining that the bidding had gotten out of control and they were going to decide by drawing straws! There were three other well-funded investors also involved in the bidding and we were all looking at the same house. Each of us had a renovation crew outside ready to go. My mother asked how high should we bid. When I asked her what was the bidding at, she said $165,000. I knew that the highest number we wanted to bid was $150,000, so I told her to leave. With all the competition and the prices bidding up so high, I realized that prices had gotten out of control and the numbers did not make sense anymore. We needed to find a new area to "farm." By the time I would have fixed that property and turned it around, if I could not sell it and had to rent it out, the rental income would not have covered or justified the expenses.

The bottom line is this: I learned to stick to my

pre-determined number. So we sold off all our assets and ventured out to look for an undiscovered area where prices made sense and where properties were affordable. Remember, we didn't have a ton of money and we could not compete with those other well-funded investors at the time.

So we got into our respective cars, and I drove to one side of the state while my mother headed to the other, seeking untapped real estate markets. Eventually we met near the middle of the state in response to a tiny ad my mother found in a local newspaper advertising new homes for only $75,000. When we arrived, we met a great local builder who was lousy at marketing. Lucky for me, I am a lousy builder but great at marketing. It was a perfect match, and our partnership was formed. I gave the builder a contract for all forty homes he was building in a subdivision. At the time, he had only five built, all of which were not sold. I took those properties on the condition that whatever I sold it for above his $75,000 asking price, I would keep. He agreed, and our ad campaign began. Flyers were circulated touting such gems as:

"Why rent when you can own?"

"Fire your landlord!"

"Low-down, easy monthly payments."

Thus we specifically targeted potential buyers who were currently renting. By teaming up with mortgage brokers, community banks, and other financing avenues, we were able to offer prospective buyers low-down, easy monthly payments tailored to their specific financial ability.

We inundated rental communities with flyers and mailers showing people how they can have a slice of the American Dream. The homes were to sell for $98,900. We sold out in just six months. And we sold some for even more money! We made approximately $25,000 per house, which is about one million dollars...all without lifting a hammer. *Ah! The art of money making money!*

I was a millionaire by the age of nineteen. We helped to facilitate the loan, get the buyer insurance, and when necessary even worked on repairing the person's credit so they could get a loan before the home was finished being constructed. We also emphasized financial counseling and education, teaching the buyers money-management skills that were never taught to them in school. For me, this was one of the most rewarding parts.

During the construction phase, we were pouring five to six foundations a week. Material was hard to acquire and the building boom was on! The homes took less than five weeks to complete, after which I began to acquire more land to build more houses and repeat the formula. The construction wasn't the hard part; closing it was. Even with the appraisal, and the insurance and all of our ducks in a row, it still could take another ten weeks or more to get the loan funded by the banks. It was as far from buying a car as you can get. They always blamed the elusive "underwriters" or some other unseen force, but at the end of the day, the delays equaled a lot of money out of our pocket.

But what I learned was priceless.

With all the newfound money my builder made, he bought himself a brand new truck: a Ford F350 King Ranch with all the bells and whistles. He walked into a dealership and drove it out the same day. He explained to me that all he had to do at the dealership was sign and drive. He said, "Wouldn't it be great if buying a home was that easy? I was out of the dealership in a couple of hours...financing and all." And that got me thinking. The idea fermented in my mind over the next several years and planted the seeds that eventually laid the foundation for the Buy Here Pay Here Real Estate System.

Why did we need to create an alternative source of financing? So what if it took a few extra weeks for the banks to close? Eventually they did close. I went on to build more than 100 homes and transacted over 1,000 pieces of real estate. In early 2008, I received a letter from the local bank where I had a large line of credit. They were pulling my line of credit along with everyone else's. I called the bank in shock and demanded to speak with the president. He said, "Larry, it isn't you. You have been a wonderful customer and you always paid on time. We are pulling everyone's line of credit. The lending world has changed forever." And so the lending crash began.

Necessity is the mother of creation and invention. And the necessity for lending brought on the creation of the Buy Here Pay Here Real Estate System.

Which came first? The lending crash or the real estate crash? To me the answer is clear: it was the lending crash that triggered the real estate crash. How do I know this? Once my line of credit was pulled, I still had homes under construction with buyers under contract. So what happened to them? When my line of credit was pulled, so was my buyer's ability to buy because they could no longer borrow. This proved to me in a very tangible way that:

Financing is the lifeblood of real estate and our economy.

The demand for affordable housing is on the rise. And the demand for affordable housing never dried up—in fact, it never really does.

People always need an affordable place to live.

As my mentor, and philanthro-capitalist, Frank McKinney, a.k.a. the "Real Estate Artist" for his multi-million dollar oceanfront spec mansions, taught me, "Since before the Roman Era there has always been very rich and very poor people. It's the people in the middle that seem to get squeezed."

So with no financing available to my buyers (and to so many other buyers from real estate to cars to consumer debt, etc.), even banks stopped lending to banks, causing the largest bank panic and shut-down in U.S. history and a world that we have not seen since the great depression. So what were I and so many others to do?

Having wealth and youth on my side, I strongly considered going back to school so I could get an education in a skill-specific profession or trade. This way I could get a job like so many others do. I then used my litmus test, which is, if I won $100 million dollars in the lottery, would I still do that job? The answer was a resounding *NO*. I encourage you to use this same litmus test to discover your true passion. We will delve into this deeply in Chapter 3.

So in an effort to be true to myself, I sold off the remaining homes and began developing a business system for real estate that would bypass the lender and bring lending back to its roots, which was peer-to-peer lending, but on a more intimate level. What I call "intimate investing," as referred to in Chapter 1, creates a real estate business system that focuses not only on putting buyers and sellers together, but putting buyers and lenders together. To date, I have bought and sold millions of dollars in real estate using the BHPH Real Estate System.

CHAPTER 3

LEARNING AND EARNING

Even though I couldn't stand being held captive in educational institutions, I always knew learning was important.

My definition of education is the practice of learning useful things. But is that what school is really about? Since my school days, I have neither had to calculate the circumference of a circle, nor had to use the Pythagorean Theorem. Why do educational institutions fill our heads with what appears to be useless and irrelevant knowledge, instead of focusing on teaching us useful things like how to balance a checkbook? Or useful technical skills such as how to change a tire, paint a wall, or fix a leaky faucet? These are practical things I believe many of us have needed to know since we left school. School is an institution where we learn to read and write, which transforms us into literate individuals. But education does not end with school—it is a lifelong process. Self-learning and personal enlightenment begin at the point that marks the end of institutional education.

Rather than leaving you floundering with no clear direction as to how to proceed, my business system gives you clear, concise, and easy to understand methods to achieve great financial success.

It is an indisputable fact that student debt is rising at an insurmountable rate, at the same time more and more college students are failing to graduate in four years.

In fact, students with weak academic records should be informed of studies indicating that out of all freshmen who attend four-year colleges having graduated in the bottom forty percent of their high school class, two-thirds of them will not graduate, even if given eight and a half years to do so. Time is a precious commodity, and many young adults are giving up years of irreplaceable time.

For the ones who defy the odds, they will most likely graduate not only with a low GPA but also having majored in a job sector that is in low demand by employers. Furthermore, it has been shown that doing well in college requires skills of linguistic and mathematical abilities that only ten to fifteen percent of our country's youth possesses.

This does not mean that only ten to fifteen percent should go on to a higher education beyond high school but it does mean that the four-year program leading to a B.A. may be the wrong model for a large majority of people.

Seventy percent of high school graduates go to college, up from forty percent in 1970. However, employers are farming out many jobs overseas, or cutting jobs to part-time, or temping out as many jobs as possible.

And the majority of schools, even MBA programs, do not teach you how to invest your money.

Yet students are finding themselves burdened by tens of thousands of dollars in educational debt, with virtually no guarantee that they will come out with any type of job to pay off that debt, let alone take care of their personal living expenses.

This begs the question: does the astronomical expense of college education justify the investment?

My personal mantra is that I prefer "deeds on the wall," not "degrees on the wall." A real estate investor can create a wealth of financial opportunities using the various deeds to properties they own, whereas degrees from colleges or universities often put your financial future at the mercy of whatever the economic climate may be.

Most colleges teach few useful job skills. Their main role is to mold hard-working conformists. It encourages people to spend many wasteful years in college, depriving the economy of millions of years of production. There is little connection between the skills students acquire in college and the skills actually needed later in life.

The path to financial success is a closely guarded secret by those in the upper echelons of society. In actuality, breeding a culture of workhorses keeps the elite few at the top of the financial ladder — the so-called vilified one percent — while bogging down the workforce with mundane obligations. BHPH Real Estate gives you the tools to unlock those secrets and learn how to reap financial rewards for yourself.

Choose your path wisely.

I recently embarked upon a tour throughout my home state of Florida to take the pulse of our economy and get a general sense of what is happening in the workplace. I spoke with many people from all walks of life. One shocking discovery was how many people I met who had taken jobs well below their qualifications. Along the way, I met waiters and waitress who were professionally trained as architects, teachers, and other occupations by trade, many holding master's degree, but could not get a job in their respective fields. In fact, I even know of one person who holds a master's degree in international business, yet he is working as a "cabana boy" in a resort hotel. The number of new jobs requiring a college degree is now less than the number of people graduating from universities, so more graduates are filling jobs for which they are academically overqualified.

At the end of the day, I agree that school is important. It does give you a taste of many things, but it is not the only way to learn to earn.

If you are not learning, you are not growing.

If you feel you know everything, then you are wrong. Today, technology changes daily. A year-old computer is practically considered a dinosaur. Don't become a dinosaur or else you, too, may become extinct. Think of life as a ladder: if you are not climbing, you are falling. If you stop on one rung for too long, it eventually breaks and you fall. So you always need to be climbing, moving upward.

During my last year of high school, I was bored out of my mind. While most of my friends were getting excited for what college they were going to go to and what fraternity they would join, I was thinking of ways that I could earn money the fastest and focus on my real passion, the one that yields the most return: making money that makes money. So I set out on an educational odyssey. I bought and listened to every book on tape I could get my hands on related to business and investing. Ultimately, I am a hybrid of them all. And as I mentioned previously, many of these books can be found online at www.LarryBieda.com.

I don't believe that everybody is made for college. After a few weeks, I dropped out. While in high school, I was able to beg and borrow to buy my first foreclosure. And real estate became my passion. A lot of books that I read did not necessarily lie, but they certainly did not disclose the full truth.

Ultimately, not everyone is cut out to be a full-time real estate investor, or importer-exporter, or day-trading stock guru or whatever the author of the week may be preaching. I have read the stock-trading books and the get-rich-quick books. I chose real estate because it was something in my DNA. And as shelter is such a basic, primordial need, it's probably in yours, too. What is more basic than having a roof over your head? A few years ago, it was a national quest—an affordable home for all—until greed took over and the lending market went berserk.

Real estate has always appealed to me. So in an effort to be true to myself, I pursued that passion and it has never steered me wrong. I encourage you to do the same. We need doctors and lawyers and roofers and lawn care professionals in this world. If everybody went to medical school and we were all doctors, then who would do our taxes? If we were all accounting wizards, then who would cure our illnesses?

This book is not about what you do for money, or how far you take your education. Rather, I advocate you take your education as far as you are comfortable with, then start to focus on using that education to make as much money as you can, saving as much as possible. And ultimately, invest what you save for income and growth for your future. Because in the end...

**It doesn't matter what you earn,
it matters what you keep!**

It doesn't matter if you are a roofer or a doctor. I know roofers who make six figures and doctors who make five figures. I also know some people who dread the idea of sitting in an office all day. On the flip side, I know people who would hate being on a roof all day. Ultimately, doctors need roofers and roofers need doctors. We gladly pay for goods and services when they are needed.

Now, many people stop here because they think saving and investing are too difficult.

But if a 10-year-old can do it, then you can do it. Whether via a lemonade stand, a lawn business, or whatever business you may choose, the point is you are selling your time, whether for $100 an hour, $10 an hour or even $1 an hour — it doesn't matter. Whether you're providing a service, creating a product, or flipping one, there is no trick to earning. Want to be a doctor? Put in the eight plus years of education. But before you waste precious time, be honest with yourself: do you really want to be a doctor, or do you just want to be rich?

Which takes us back to my litmus test mentioned briefly earlier:

If you won $100 million dollars in the lottery tomorrow, would you still want to be doing the same thing?

My answer is yes...what is yours?

Be true to yourself.

Earning doesn't only mean making money. Earning also means receiving: donating your time as a volunteer or offering up your talent and treasure for others to benefit from. This type of earning fulfills you in a way that reaches far beyond your materialistic needs and offers a unique gratification in an emotional and spiritual way. Because after all, isn't your end goal, no matter how much money you earn, being happy?

CHAPTER 4

SAVING AND INVESTING

In order to understand the importance of savings and investing, we must first take a brief look at the history of banking to appreciate how it relates to us today.

Banking began in the Middle Ages. The first banks were merchant banks, created by Italian grain merchants. It soon progressed from financing trade on one's own behalf to settling trades for others and then to holding deposits for the settlement of notes written by the people who brokered the grain. People gave their money to money-lenders, thus marking the beginning of the *peer-to-peer* monetary system. This system has grown into the international banking system we know today.

The money-lenders set up their stalls in the middle of enclosed courtyards on long benches called *bancu*, from which the word bank is derived. So the merchant's "benches" were considered the first banks. They were held in public places, in markets, at fairs, etc., where they tallied their money. If a banker failed, he broke his bank. Interestingly, the word bankrupt is derived from the Italian word *banca rotta*, or broken bench, which is what happened when someone lost his traders' deposits and thus was "broke."

Banks may be referred to as several different entities. A central bank circulates money on behalf of a government and enacts monetary policy that regulates the money supply. A commercial bank accepts deposits and pools those funds to provide credit either by directly lending funds, or indirectly by investing funds through the capital markets. Finally, a savings bank can either be stockholder owned or mutually owned, with residential mortgage loans providing the main assets of the institution's portfolio.

Overall, a bank's main source of revenue is derived from interest income. Banks pay out at a lower rate on deposits and receive a higher interest rate on loans. The difference between these rates represents the bank's net income.

Throughout the years, banking has changed in many ways. Today, financial institutions offer a wide range of products and services and deliver them faster and more efficiently than ever before. Up until recently, their central function remained the same: putting a community's excess funds (deposits and investments) to work by lending to people to buy homes or cars, to start or expand a business, to obtain a college education, etc.

Historically, banks have been viewed as vital to the health of our nation's economy, often being the first choice for saving, borrowing and investment. But in an economic downturn, where countries face unprecedented debt—and millions of people face losing their homes, tremendous job losses, and the erosion of their way of life—not only has the game changed, but the rules have changed as well.

Gone are the days where you could rely on the bank for a loan.

The fact is, banks have been the recipients of loans from taxpayers in the form of government bailouts. We need to rely on our own ingenuity and creative thinking to replace the traditional way of doing business. That is the beauty of BHPH Real Estate, which was born out of the need to replace the bank.

BHPH Real Estate replaces conventional financing with creative financing while putting the buyer's and the investor's needs at a parallel.

My method teaches how buyers can tap into lenders, and how investors can virtually print paper money with incredible returns, as I will demonstrate to you in Chapter 8. Saving and investing are two integral concepts to master in order to achieve financial success.

Now, I do not necessarily agree with the philosophy of cutting up your credit cards and living like a pauper. Being cheap does not mean you have a high IQ. It actually doesn't take much intelligence at all to save. If you think about it, even a squirrel knows how to save: they take some acorns and stash them away for the winter. So I am not going to teach you how to save. People don't save because they lack the know-how; the masses generally understand the simplicity of just living on less than what you bring in. It is that straightforward.

I believe that what most people lack is the motivation to save.

It is funny that most people who save usually are saving for something, whether it is a car, a video game or whatever, because they want that fast return, that instant gratification or reward. Saving in banks or bonds, or giving it to a stockbroker and hoping for the best, is just not exciting.

Not surprisingly, it is a fact that spending money gives people an emotional "high." Marketers and branding experts have spent millions of dollars fine-tuning this practice. They know how to prey on your emotions so that buying a sports car, an expensive cell phone or high-definition television becomes an integral part of how you define who you are and how you stack up against your neighbors, instead of becoming what it really is: a negative cash-flow situation.

One of the ways they give you that emotional high for buying things that just depreciate and create negative-cash-flow situations is by providing you easy access to those types of deals.

BHPH Real Estate solves this problem because it creates an investment high for people by providing easy access to investing and buying regardless of what level buyer or investor you are, whether you are an end-user, landlord, or flipper.

The emotional high you get in purchasing items also brings a certain feeling of status...that you belong, and have reached a certain level of success by owning name-brand products. Think about it. How many times in a conversation have you heard people refer to their cell phone as an iPhone? The same holds true for Apple laptops. The company does not simply call it a laptop, but a MacBook. Apple products make great examples because they are amazing at emotional branding. Look at how many people line up in advance to be one of the first to receive their new products.

When you buy something based on emotion, you are more likely to refer to it by its brand name. It is a subtle way for you to get the point across that you spent a lot of money on a particular item, and that must make you more successful, fashionable or beautiful, and even a more interesting person! Society buys into the emotional marketing blitz because they want us to believe that having more "stuff" will bring us happiness. But just the opposite is true. When the credit card bill arrives, we find ourselves more depressed than ever. And what does this teach our children?

We need to set an example and show how saving and investing brings a sense of satisfaction as well as financial stability and success.

The answer lies not in how to be more frugal, but in how to utilize the BHPH Real Estate System. This business method teaches you the strategies needed to save and invest wisely. Product marketers have mastered emotional branding, but savers and investors ignore those emotional overtones and focus on the numbers.

As I often say, "I don't fall in love with the house, I fall in love with the deal."

Let's say, for example, that you buy a new car for $30,000 and finance it at $300 a month. If you had invested that money instead, it could have returned $300 a month, every month for the rest of your life. Instead, you are left with a depreciating asset that may or may not last you approximately eight years before it will have to be replaced, all with nothing to show for it! Now, consider if you had to purchase that same $30,000 car with no financing. Who would get an emotional high from that? How many people actually have $30,000 to purchase a car outright? But when it is packaged with terms such as, "low-down" and "easy monthly payments," people jump at it.

The same holds true for real estate.

You can sell a $30,000 unit, a $100,000 condominium, or a $1 million home, if you make it palatable, accessible, exciting, and convenient for people to buy.

Now I have read plenty of books on savings and some are quite helpful. By now you know the drill. You can find all of the books I studied on my personal blog at www.LarryBieda.com. Savings has been around as long as there has been money. It hasn't changed. The only thing that has changed are our returns. But investing has changed significantly. Between online stock trading and mortgages being bundled up and sold as CDOs (collateralized debt obligations), the business of investing is now global. Many countries have their own exchanges so you can trade twenty-four hours a day, and money moves at the speed of light.

The monetary system has become so complicated, many people do not truly know where to put their money, where it goes, and if it's safe. Look at all of the daunting options. What is a 401(k)? What is an IRA (Individual Retirement Account)? What is a mutual fund, an ETF (Exchange Traded Fund) or a Treasury bill? I don't remember being taught any of this lingo in school. It's funny how in tough economic times people run to the simplest investments such as gold, silver and other commodities, things that they understand. They do this because the truth is, they did not understand what they were investing in before. They just gave their money over blindly hoping it would appreciate for reasons ultimately unknown to them.

We were never taught to invest or how much fun it could be, so why save to invest?

"Just save to spend" is what we were taught. This problem is exemplified in our national debt crisis. Whole countries are spending for today and not thinking about tomorrow. This trend is nothing new, as history seems to repeat itself. In fact, it is often said that one of the best reasons to study history is to help shed some light on today's circumstances. In order to predict the future direction of the housing market or the stock market, it is common to start by looking at the past because, in most cases, the trends often repeat themselves. And while it is true that the past performance of any market can never guarantee future returns, most investors still tend to look backward.

I encourage you to turn your head around and look toward the future!

BHPH Real Estate has a proven track record that takes the guesswork out of investing. No studying trends and no relying on historical events. We make it easy to learn and put into practice. Most importantly, we make it convenient by offering a one-stop shopping experience that traverses any market condition, high or low.

We don't speculate if the prices go up or down—it doesn't matter. Either way, we do not have a crystal ball. Our main business is cash flow with a belief and understanding that value can be created or destroyed via the presence of or lack of financing.

Financial advisors preach diversification, which I often refer to as "deworsification" (making your financial portfolio less worse...LOL!). In all seriousness, I agree with the idea of diversifying, as long as it is done right. However diversifying in the stock market is not enough. I believe that you need to also have money earmarked for real estate investing and money earmarked that you control. Invest and pray for the best is NOT a good financial plan.

You can either use leverage or be leverage for someone else...the choice is up to you.

To leverage or be leveraged? It all depends on your risk tolerance. I believe that the best place to invest is in real estate because wealth that is kept in the form of currency can be easily stolen, whereas investing in real estate is obviously much more secure.

If nothing else, I want this book to excite you about investing because if you are excited about investing, then you will be excited about savings, which means you will have something to invest. I want you to see how fun it is. The idea of being a passive investor and just giving it to a stockbroker and hoping for the best would bore me, too.

No wonder why the average person does not have enough savings to retire.

Because you have not been taught how to invest, the government has created investment programs that force you to invest through withholdings called the Social Security program. But ultimately, they don't know what to do with the money because the government is in bigger trouble than we are. Would you take the advice of or give your money to a stockbroker who is trillions of dollars in debt? That is what you do every month. What do you call a system where the oldest or longest-term investors get paid out dividends from investments of the new investors? I call that a Ponzi scheme! Bernie Madoff was small potatoes compared to dear old Uncle Sam!

I am not saying this to scare you, but to prepare you for what is to come.

In 2005, I was in Panama City, Panama, at a banking and investment summit. I was sitting next to a very nice gentleman who engaged me in conversation. He asked me, "What do you do?" I told him real estate development. He said, "We are in the same business." I replied, "Oh really? You too? What do you specialize in, residential or commercial?" He said, "No, we are in the same business, but not selling the same product. Your business is buying real estate at one price and selling at another. I do the same thing, but I do it with shoes. I buy them at one price and sell them at another price."

Ah!! The art of money making money!

When you invest money in a publicly traded company in the stock market, they use it for many things, all of which you have no control over. They may choose to use it for research and development or building inventory or paying their CEOs hundreds of millions of dollars between salaries and bonuses. When you put your money into a bank, whether it is a savings account, money market, CD or whatever, ultimately, the bank is using your money to lend out to other people and you have no say or knowledge in where it goes or how it is used. The investment system is based on trust, and too many people rely on blind trust. That is how fraud becomes rampant.

It is your responsibility to know where your money is going and have control over your investments.

The difference between investing and speculating is that speculators follow the "buy, hold and pray" theory and hope prices go up. But in my definition:

Investing is when you know what your return is the moment you enter that investment.

Because it operates on this principle, BHPH Real Estate shows you *exactly* how to become successful at investing and making money in real estate.

CHAPTER 5

WHY REAL ESTATE?

As I mentioned before...

More wealth has been created in real estate than in any other investment in history.

In case that is not reason enough, I'll reveal the main reason I like real estate...

**You are able to add value to it —
and you have control over it.**

Adding value is all about perception, or what I call perceived value. I can truly make an $8,000 kitchen look like a $40,000 kitchen. But the right combination of granite and stainless steel appliances is only one example of that. Paint goes a long way — whereas you cannot paint your stocks and bonds or stare at your gold, willing it to go up in value. To this day, it blows my mind that in some areas you can buy a quarter-acre lot that has water, sewer and fifty-plus feet of road frontage with twenty pine trees and scrub on it for the same price as an ounce of gold. And what can you do to that ounce of gold to bring up its value? Nothing. Oftentimes people ask me why the stock market went up today. My answer is simple: there were more buyers than sellers. But this changes from day to day.

Rather than living with this brand of uncertainty, I enjoy investments that you can drive by and wave at, and if worst comes to worst, you can always just pop a tent and live on them. People ask "What if you buy one piece of real estate and then the price drops in half?" My advice is: if it was a good deal when you bought it, then it is still a good deal at half the price.

Why? Because you can dollar-cost average. For example, if you bought one deal for $100,000 and it was a good deal, then another deal at $50,000, then you have brought the purchase price for each unit to $75,000 per unit. This is called dollar-cost averaging. Construction costs today, depending on where you live, can range anywhere from between $75 to $100 per square foot and more, not including the land. So purchasing a 2,000-square-foot house for $50,000 just makes sense to me. You cannot even build it for $25 per square foot, let alone figuring in the cost of the land.

Let's say you own a stock. Can you rent it out? Do you have any control over your investment? Just for fun, I have always wanted to walk into a company I own a share of, and start demanding that they use less paper, cut costs or work more efficiently. But obviously you cannot do that. These companies are so big, your money is barely a drop in the bucket.

Real estate gives you the opportunity to become an inside investor and to create the deal. When I knew that people needed affordable housing, I created that opportunity for them. I sold what sells and what was needed. Everyone needs and deserves a good, affordable roof over their head.

What is the definition of affordable housing?

I looked it up and it was quite confusing. When I was a kid, I was always taught that when defining a word you cannot use the word you are defining in the definition. And basically the definition went something like this: "Affordable housing is housing that is affordable." Duh! Other definitions go on to give you median home prices and other unrelated data and statistics.

My definition is simple: affordable housing is when it is cheaper or the same price to buy as it is to rent.

It does not mean living in slums or bad neighborhoods. For example, if you live in a home that would cost you $2,000 a month if you were to rent it, and instead you own it, and your mortgage is $2,000 or less, then you live in affordable housing. Ultimately, everyone wants to own the roof over their head. Rent you have to pay forever, but eventually, you will pay off a 30-year mortgage, and even if you live there for only five years, at least you have paid down something toward the principle, while entering a utopia called equity. Who wants to be answerable to a landlord? Who doesn't want to live in Utopia? After all, owning your own home is the American Dream.

My real estate investment philosophy has never been based on the idea that real estate prices go up no matter what. Prices go up and prices go down. So when I was buying during the real estate boom, my investments were fueled by low interest rates and loose lending that was encouraged after the horrific terrorist attack on September 11, 2001, in order to stimulate our economy. If I still held those investments today, even now they would be good deals. You may ask, "Why? Didn't the prices go down in the areas you bought? Didn't you get affected by the crash?" Sure, prices went down, but I was not buying for appreciation alone.

Buying for appreciation alone is not investing, it is speculating.

I buy for cash flow. Besides, rents rarely go down. With every property that I buy, I have one question about that property: "What are you going to do with it?"

Buying a quarter-acre lot in the middle of nowhere because it is cheap is not necessarily what I advocate.

Investing with specific purpose is what I advocate.

Ultimately, nobody wants to be a landlord and take on all of the headaches that go along with it. I like having hair on my head. I don't enjoy the phone calls at 2:00 a.m., and I no longer deal with them. I have spent many years perfecting my investing techniques and creating the BHPH Real Estate System. I have eliminated everything people don't like about real estate such as management headaches, vacancies, and repairs...just to name a few, and of course the dreaded one...eviction! I have created a real estate business system enhanced with all the conveniences that have been keeping people investing in the stock market: that is just like the "set-it and forget-it" management of their money. But unlike stocks, bonds, mutual funds, etc., real estate is tangible, solid and real. You can touch it. Its occupants are living, breathing organisms and it is a moving target. So until now, "set-it and forget-it" real-estate investment has not been possible.

Where did the American Dream go?

Why did people line up during the real estate boom to buy $200,000 condos and when those same condos are selling for $50,000 no one is around to buy them?

Where have all the buyers gone? The truth is...the buyers are still here. I know many people who want to buy.

Then are there no sellers? Are you kidding? Of course there are plenty of sellers! Look around and you will see that neighborhoods are littered with foreclosures and for-sale signs, and banks are flooded with inventory. So if it is not the buyers or the sellers, then what is missing?

It is the lenders.

They have all left the party where the fire they ignited nearly burned down our economy.

You see, the need for affordable housing as I define it, never dried up. Why rent when you can own? Most of my buyers were previous renters. They are realizing the American Dream, climbing the ladder rung by rung. I can still build the same houses, but for what reason? There are properties I can pick up for a fraction of actual construction costs, and even those are still not selling. The piece of the equation that is missing is the lending component. A willing buyer and willing seller alone does not a closing make!

We need willing lenders. Ultimately banks are not lending at a pace that meets the demand.

I recently saw a condo that was a bank foreclosure for $25,000 and it was a so-so deal at that price. Sure it makes money, but do I really want the hassle of buying the unit and tying up $25,000? So I offered the bank $50,000 for their $25,000 unit with one catch...I wanted them to finance the purchase with only 10 percent down, which is $5,000, and finance the rest at 6 percent interest.

Within a few days, I received a reply from the bank's agent saying that the bank does not want to finance this property. I was shocked. I thought that banks were in the business of lending money! And after all, the reason why the bank had to take the unit back is because they lent someone else a crazy amount of money on it. Most foreclosures are not because of job loss. Most foreclosures are because of the loss in equity. Let's face it, everything is for sale! If the property were worth

$1 million dollars more than they paid for it, they most likely would sell it.

Here's how "Buy Here Pay Here" financing can make a good deal great.

I have spent many years looking at countless deals, analyzing them, doing an astounding amount of due diligence on many properties, and understanding the components of what makes a good deal great.

Some years ago, I purchased forty acres of beautiful pine-scented property consisting of gently rolling hills, sprinkled with an abundance of wild orange, lemon and grapefruit trees. I was able to buy the property through owner financing. I bought it for $10,000 per acre, with little money down and at a decent interest rate. I ended up selling the less desirable parcel that had less road frontage for $20,000 per acre, and provided my own owner financing to the purchaser with 30 percent down, and at a healthy 10 percent interest rate. The loan was for five years, which netted me an additional profit of almost $150,000 in interest alone, and that was just on the back end of the parcel. I was able to sell off the remaining twenty acres with owner financing, and when all was said and done, by offering creative financing, I was able to essentially create paper money out of thin air, and ended up with a $1 million profit. If the buyers defaulted, then I would have enacted the cardinal rule of BHPH Real Estate: *"No Pay, No Stay."* I take great pride in the fact that with my expertise, I am able to build solid deals that are win-win-win situations for all parties involved: a winning deal for the lender, a winning deal for the buyer, and a winning deal for the investor.

I would like to share with you another great example of creative financing on both the acquisition and sale of over 400 residential lots, many of which had no roads, water or electricity to the site. On the acquisition side, with a purchase price of $3,500,000, I had to knock on a lot of doors to get the initial financing in place. It took a lot of persistence and patience to say the least, and enabled me to hone my skills on how to approach people when asking for a loan. But one vital aspect, which is very important for you to have when approaching people, is to exude enthusiasm, confidence and your belief in what you are selling. It makes the "pitch" that much smoother.

You see, you must be able to sell yourself first on an idea before you solicit anyone else. If people can feel your excitement, most often they will want to jump on the bandwagon and have a piece of the action.

Once the purchase was made, I immediately put half of the property on the market and sold it for double the price. That meant that the remainder of the property was essentially free and clear of any debt. When I did find a buyer for the remainder of the property, I took a sizeable down payment, charged a fair interest rate, and held a $2.8 million mortgage with owner financing. The exciting part is that I created the $2.8 million on paper. Thus, the profit I made, combined with the interest on the note, translated into a sizeable return. I worked hard to build a solid deal that was a win-win-win for all involved:

- **the purchaser** was thrilled because he bought many contiguous lots that he would be able to develop into a beautiful housing subdivision.

- **my lenders** were all paid back in full with interest, and

- **my partners and I** were rewarded with a stantial profit.

Subsequently, I went on to repeat this formula again and again, and I discovered that when offering creative financing, it is essential to be innovative and resourceful, especially when putting buyers and lenders together. Think about how much money a bank will lend you on a house versus how much they will lend you to invest in a stock, bond, or mutual fund. It is estimated that an average of eighty percent of new companies go out of business within the first five years. You can insure your real estate against nearly any risk, but you can't insure your stock portfolio.

When all is said and done, real estate investment is the best vehicle for wealth creation. And that is why I like real estate.

The tools and techniques I used to buy and sell my properties — and yes, even unload them in a bad market when other financing options were not present — is what gave me the vision for BHPH Real Estate.

CHAPTER 6

WHAT LENDERS, BUYERS AND INVESTORS NEED TO KNOW

Let me start by giving my definition of a real estate buyer. Oftentimes we refer to a buyer as an investor, but I do not believe that your home or vacation home is an investment. If it is your largest investment, then you are in trouble. A buyer is someone who purchases real estate as an end-user to either live in or use as a vacation home, rents it out for cash flow as a landlord, or purchases it with the intent to resell it as a flipper.

Even if you have money in the bank, eventually there is a pretty good chance that you will run out. Corporations borrow, governments borrow, even banks borrow, so why shouldn't you? In an economy fueled by financing, the idea and dream of being debt-free is often not a reality. To compensate for this reality, BHPH Real Estate is all about putting the lenders, buyers and investors together.

Many investors and financial planners alike have this notion that real estate is what you live in while stocks, bonds and mutual funds are what you invest in.

Society's institutions also allow you to list the cash you have in the bank as an asset, even though it is depreciating. I don't think your cash is not an asset, but if it really is to you, why let it sit rotting in the bank, losing value?

There are plenty of people who want to borrow on good, qualified deals for good qualified buyers. So as a lender you are in the catbird's seat: people bring deals to you, and you get to choose whether to give them the thumbs up or down. You can also syndicate a deal (take part of a deal).

As a lender, you get to make the rules.

I was recently offered a deal: a man needed a $30,000 loan for a home he just purchased for $100,000. He offered me 15 percent interest and his plan was to repay me in twelve months by refinancing the loan. After doing my due diligence, both the buyer and the appraisal checked out. But quite frankly, I did not want to do the deal. If it went bad, I did not want to be in a situation where I could be tied up in a foreclosure case over $30,000. That is the reason why people don't want to do small deals; they are too small.

But I consider myself to be a "deal maker," not a "deal breaker." So instead of asking how many ways this deal could go wrong, I asked how can it go right? My creative financing juices kicked in and I proposed that the deal should stay at the 15 percent for twelve months, but instead of holding a mortgage for him, which would have left me vulnerable to a possible foreclosure if he were to stop paying, my proposition was that if he were so sincere about paying back the loan, then he should "sell" me the property...title it over to me in exchange for the $30,000 and every month continue to pay me the 15 percent on the money as an option fee. He would be given a contract to purchase it back on or before the twelve months. What I basically did was turn the tables on him and make sure I was secured in giving the loan. Remember this BHPH Real Estate Golden Rule:

He who has the title makes the rules, just as he who has the gold makes the rules.

My terms, although steep, insured the safety of my money. Already having ownership to the property versus just giving a loan eliminates the necessity of ever having to foreclose because you don't have to foreclose on a property you already own. I view every dollar as a soldier working for me. I would never send any of my soldiers into battle knowing that they would not come back. I want to ensure their success. Ultimately, the terms were accepted and I funded the deal through a syndication, putting multiple partners together and taking a piece of the action for myself.

This is just an example of many deals and many strategies that are available to the lender. Finding deals is very easy: you just have to let people know you are in the market and they will follow. Build your contacts with like-minded people who identify with the BHPH Real Estate culture, and who love their money more than they love their stockbrokers.

There are countless resources that will help you lend out your money safely and securely that can be found on the Internet and many other places. If they don't exist and you don't find what you need, create it, whether it is:

- **an angel investing fund:** an angel investor is typically a wealthy individual or group of individuals who provide capital for a business or real estate acquisition or joint venture. Often, angel investors share research and pool their investment capital.

- **a private placement fund:** a private placement fund is usually a small number of select investors who pool their funds to raise capital.

- **a venture capital fund:** a venture capitalist provides financial capital to start-up companies with high potential and high risk. The fund makes money by owning equity in the company they invest in, and often has control over company decisions in addition to a large portion of the company's ownership. A venture capital fund is attractive for new companies that are too small to raise money in the public markets or cannot get a bank loan.

- **a lending club:** a group of people joining together lending peer-to-peer.

- or just a bunch of people putting their money into a "kitty" to beat the market's return. Everyone shares the same goal: to have their money work for them as hard as possible, instead of them working hard for their money.

And investors, you need to learn the fine art of pitch building.

Never be afraid to ask. If you do not ask, you certainly will not get. If the answer could be yes or no, if you do not ask, then the answer is one hundred percent no. However if you do ask, you automatically increase your odds and have a 50/50 chance of getting a positive response. Be persistent and be shameless about it. Ultimately you are providing the potential lender with a great opportunity as well.

Think of as many ways as you can to protect the lender and to make them feel warm and fuzzy. Try imagining that you are the lender being pitched the deal. Ask yourself, is it something that you would accept? Remember the adage to "do unto others are you would have others do unto you." So be sure to offer the deal to others that you yourself would want to have offered to you. I believe that the world is round: if you want a punch, give a punch; if you want a smile, then give a smile. If you want a good deal, give someone else a good deal in return. What goes around comes around.

And don't discriminate against small lenders.

If a lender indicates that they only have $5,000 to invest, figure out how the deal would work with their $5,000 even if you need $100,000. Twelve percent on $5,000 is far better than zero percent. I will state the obvious...the higher the interest rate, the better. The more points, the better — and make sure you have a viable, reasonable and coherent plan to pay your indebtedness. Oftentimes you can offer to give the lender a piece of the action and in return, you can lower the interest rate. Be creative. Have all of your ducks in a row. Be mindful of the three "C's" of lending: *credibility, collateral* and *character*. And finally, know what you need: appraisals, credit scores, financial statements, Phase I environmental reports, executive summaries, etc.

What if you don't know anyone with money? Surely you know someone. If not, hit the Internet search engines and type in the words "hard money lender." Thousands of resources should come up. Call, email and repeat. Find solutions, not obstacles, to obtaining what you need. Ask people who work for people who have money if they have clients who are interested in making money. Accountants deal with people who have money all the time and often know people who are investors.

If you are involved in a church, synagogue or any type of affiliation for that matter, you probably know people who are big donors. Hang where the money hangs. I knew someone who used to go to a car wash that had a lot of high-end exotic cars. He always had his pitch in hand to network and meet contacts. Ultimately, if you are too shy to ask, put it in an email. Then call to follow up on the email. It takes too much time to pitch person-to-person. With the click of the mouse and a blind copy, you can send it to many people; and you can link it to your Facebook, Twitter, LinkedIn and other social networking resources. But ultimately, you have to believe as I did: if it is a good enough deal, the money will follow.

The cup is half full and the opportunity is now here. The relationship between lenders, buyers and investors is important to the implementation of the BHPH Real Estate System and philosophy. After all, we are in the business of putting lenders, buyers and investors together.

Finding deals is a very important step for an investor. Realtors, brokers and other professionals are very good at what they do, but you have to ask the right questions and know what you are looking for. If you walked into a car dealership, you need to know what you want...a car, an SUV, a van, two doors, four doors, etc. Many times you may not find the perfect real estate agent or professional at first. They often focus on curb appeal and lovely wall colors versus the "bottom-line" numbers. Be persistent and relentless until you find exactly the right person who understands what you are looking for.

Most importantly, be mindful of one of the basic principles of the BHPH Real Estate System:

Don't fall in love with the house,
fall in love with the deal!

Remember the three "L's"...location, location, location. You can change anything about the property but not the location.

As far as your risk tolerance is concerned, be true to yourself. Once you do find the right real estate broker, the deals will just start flowing. You just need to fund them.

You do not need to be a real estate broker yourself. Sometimes, it is not worth acquiring knowledge when you can rent it, but I do believe in paying professionals and paying them well. If they are good at what they do, then I am sure they have other people looking for similar deals. Sometimes it is worth sweetening the pot by offering them an extra percentage or bonus to encourage them to send more deals your way. You may want to find someone who specializes in foreclosures, also known as REOs (real estate owned), land, commercial, etc. I also ask them to print out or email over listings that are under $25,000 and in a certain area, then keep bumping it up depending on market conditions. They also can perform CMAs (comparative market analysis) to give you a good understanding of the market, as well as comps. All of these services are provided on success-based pay. They are only paid upon a successful closing. At the end of the day, let them know you are looking for a long-lasting business relationship that is beneficial for all parties. There is no such thing as something for nothing...it has to work for everybody.

Oftentimes, you can ask real estate agents to look for deals that have assumable financing or owner financing. They are also a good resource to ask to help you find lenders and investors. Because they know people in the business, they can be a vital asset.

A landlord is someone who buys real estate and rents it out and therefore is in the business of being a landlord. I think it is too vague to just say, "What do you do in real estate? Are you an investor?" It is like asking someone whether they breathe. Everyone needs to breathe and everyone needs to invest. So being specific and having a plan when you make a purchase will save you a lot of time and headaches trying to figure out who you are and what you are going to do with this new purchase. To me, investors should not have to get their hands dirty in the day-to-day operations of real estate. Real estate is a breathing organism and many things can happen to it.

Financing creates accessibility. More access means more buyers, and more buyers mean greater demand. More demand means that things can be produced in mass quantities. Quantities drive down the cost per unit creating affordability...affordable housing!

Imagine if auto financing were like real estate financing...not readily available and hard to get even for the most qualified buyer. In real estate, it takes a long time to get financed. If that were the case in the auto industry, the large auto manufacturers would have to slow down or limit production. This would raise the price per unit, creating unaffordability in the car market.

The BHPH Real Estate vision is to give access to affordable houses to the masses the same way that modern car dealerships do with cars.

My vision is to turn the business of real estate into a real estate dealership that can help and affect everyone at all levels by making it easy to do business, adding convenience for the buyer, and increasing profits for the lenders and investors.

Personally, I do not advocate leasing cars and I never have, but my company has leased cars. Let's just say the CEO needs a new set of wheels, and I do not look good in cheap cars! Leasing my car allows me to get into a new car every two to three years, and also offers a big tax advantage. Because I use my car primarily for business purposes, the cost of operating the car is deductible from my federal income tax. When I went to the car dealership, I could not believe how quickly I was in and out. The salesman gave me the keys to a brand new car for what would be the equivalent price of a condo, needing just my signature and a small down payment. What a pleasant, hassle-free and convenient way to do business.

Low-down, easy monthly payments is the way anything can be sold. It is another way that value is added. By adding financing you are also adding convenience, which is another value-add technique that I practice.

Ultimately, you want to make it easy to do business with you. As a developer during the boom, I could never understand how we were able to build a house from foundation to CO (certificate of occupancy) within five weeks but we couldn't get a bank loan for our buyers in ten weeks! And that was during the good times. Essentially, it took longer to finance than to build.

The automobile industry would not exist today as we know it if people saw a car they liked, test drove it, and had to come back in 10 weeks to buy it. And the real estate market is essentially no different. So I created sign- and-drive real estate.

Better yet, **"sign and reside"** real estate!

Anyone who says the American Dream is dead does not know what they are talking about, and anyone who says that the American Dream is only a dream also doesn't know what they are talking about. People from all walks of life want to and deserve to benefit from owning the roof over their head. A lot of people have beer budgets and wine tastes, so they never get into the game because they don't want to lower their standards and just get into the game and begin to build equity.

We all have to start somewhere.

As a young boy, I used to go to sleep-away camp and we would camp in the woods. When the nights would get cold, we would build a fire. Everyone would go out and search for firewood. Most people would drag back huge, impressive logs that were usually wet in the middle. But I would bring back small sticks and twigs. My fire would burn all night and theirs would not even start. Because you need to start a fire with small sticks and twigs...it's the snowball effect: you first have to learn to crawl before you walk and walk before you run and so on.

Ah, but we live in an age of instant gratification.

So by creating that for our buyers, BHPH Real Estate gives them the ability to get into a home quickly. The process is streamlined. Appraisals aren't necessary because we are the lenders and we know what it's worth. Credit checks are mandatory, but it comes along with credit counseling. Let's face it, our customers would not borrow from us if they could borrow from a conventional bank. And our ultimate goal is to have them refinance so we can get our money back and our profit.

But until then we will collect rent on our money, better known as interest. The interest will typically be at a higher rate than a conventional bank, but it will be affordable, meaning their payment shall never exceed what they are able to afford to pay in rent. And being that conventional banks are overwhelmingly not lending to the masses, BHPH Real Estate offers a realistic alternative.

The high interest rate will behoove the buyer to refinance and get into a much lower rate. I envision this rate at being somewhere around 12 percent. Why 12 percent? Because it is easy to figure out your payment. For example, a $100,000 mortgage is $1,000 per month; a $30,000 mortgage is $300 per month...interest only, of course. I like to keep things simple. I use the "12 percent rule" because it's easy and it's realistic. As a general rule of thumb, when figuring numbers, always figure high. So if you calculated too high then at least you have extra money left over...not a bad thing at all!

There shall be no prepayment penalties and the interest rate shall be fixed with no teaser rates. All loans will require a substantial down payment (somewhere in the range of 10 percent plus). If they do not have the down payment, we can choose to work with them on a case-by-case basis. After all, it is our real estate and we are the sellers, not the agents.

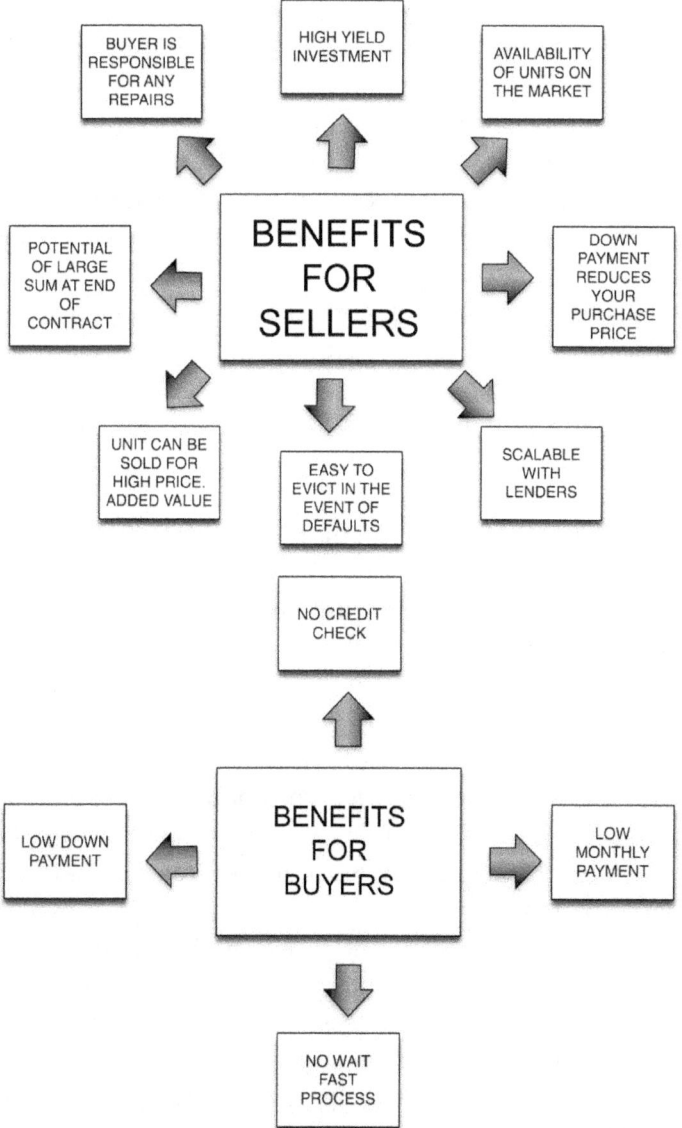

We sell to all types of buyers: owners/end users, vacation home owners, landlords and flippers. Initially, most of our buyers are coming from "Rent-to-Own" ads. They are tenants who are looking to move, have some money to put down, and did not realize they could own for the same price they can rent. This affordable pricing benefits the buyers, whether they are an owner-occupant end user, or someone wanting a vacation home, or someone who wants to be a landlord, or a flipper just looking to get his foot into the door of a property.

During a recent consultation with a client, the client said that he cannot wait to save enough money to buy a unit. In this particular case, it was a small foreclosure for $25,000 that should be able to sell for $50,000. He felt that he first needed to save $25,000 in order to do the deal. I explained that his mind-set was how the poor think. The rich don't think, how can I save in order to do a deal? They think, how can I borrow the money to get the deal done?

So why gamble money in the stock market or by guessing what a stock or a commodity will be trading at in six months from now or whatever? Especially when you now know how to double your money...on paper that is.

I believe paper money is better than real money because real money in the bank can only make a few percent in interest, but paper money is money that you hold in paper and is oftentimes your profit in the form of an "IOU." It is held at whatever interest rate you and the borrower, or in this case the buyer agrees to.

By charging 12 percent interest you certainly beat the return from a bank many times over!

I also have a vision for the investor...the person who does not want to deal with tenants, such as a professional, whether a doctor, lawyer, policeman, teacher, roofer or an individual in some other occupation.

These professionals work from nine to five, and often much later, only to come home from their job to face more work with family and personal responsibilities. This is where the BHPH Real Estate lending comes into play. The investors participate in *pools of loans* on real estate that meets their qualifications. The loans are solid because they are given to people who are proven to be able to afford them. The loans shall also be backed by the real estate "dealership" that approves the borrower, thus ensuring accountability.

In essence, the lender, buyer and investor are part of an intelligent real estate "dealership". By applying the BHPH Real Estate principles, you can be that profitable dealership and find yourself sitting squarely in the driver's seat of every deal.

If a loan fails, the "dealership" takes it back and remarkets it. Because of the lengthy foreclosure process, we suggest that you opt to hold title to the properties, giving people land contracts or contracts for deed, option contracts, or other various legal remedies that ensure that if they do not pay, they do not stay. Our upside is in the ultimate payoff of the property. But in the event that they don't pay, you evict them, take the property back, and put in a new buyer so lenders do not get tangled up in the foreclosure process. The lender also won't be involved in remarketing the property and they won't even miss a payment because it's guaranteed by the participating "dealership."

Implementing my revolutionary BHPH Real Estate business method can help, and can also affect everyone at all levels. The keys are making it easy to conduct business and adding convenience for the buyer. If, for example, the bank deems a property or buyer is not lendable due to a litany of reasons — such as the property not having viable comparative values, it not appraising out, or the buyer having a less than sterling credit score — then the BHPH Real Estate System is ideal, as it provides the ease and convenience of one-stop-shopping when purchasing properties. Ideally, distressed assets are the best deals, but the banks won't lend on them because they are distressed...which, ironically, is a situation that many of the banks created!

One of the BHPH Real Estate System's key components is to get the loan for the buyer in-house, quickly and conveniently.

Flippers: The traditional flipper is fast becoming extinct in today's new real estate market, due to the inability of the buyer to get a loan. However, by using the BHPH Real Estate System, you can actually make money on the flip. Hence, in this system, the flipper is alive and well.

Landlords: Landlords generally like holding onto their property long- term hoping that the property will significantly appreciate over time. In this case, they may enjoy long-term capital gains, while taking advantage of depreciation, cash flow and an eventual capital play, using the long-term capital gains tax strategy. The BHPH Real Estate System allows you to do all of that, but we provide the added benefit of reducing management. No more smelly toilets or leaky roofs to deal with!

Lenders: As part of the BHPH Real Estate System, the lender is completely separate from the deal. They are ready, willing and able to lend, but only fund the inventory. They do not have to actually see the property, nor do they ever need to get their hands dirty; essentially they get to use the same convenience that they enjoy by investing in stocks, bonds and mutual funds, and apply it to real estate investing. After all, that is why so many professionals and investors steered away from investing.

Until now, real estate investing was too messy. Convenience is the key, as people appreciate when it is easy to do business with you.

Remember, make that soda cold and easily accessible, and people will gladly pay double or triple for the product.

Now, you may be wondering if private-party funding and hard-money lending like this already exists. The answer is yes, but only for the very wealthy, not for the masses. Moreover, what does exist is quite fractionalized; it is not succinct. I want to open this up to people who have small amounts of money to invest, and be the "equal opportunity borrowers and lenders."

There is a unique niche for people in the lending market to lend on small deals.

I recently got a call from a broker representing a lender who was offering great rates, but only wanted to lend a minimum of $500,000. Why? Because they are paid based on commission, and are obviously short-sighted.

Why do I bother with small investors?

Because if I am truly good at what I do...and I am, then those small investors will become big investors. Your $1,000 investor will eventually become a $10,000 investor, and your $100,000 investor will become a $1 million investor. This means that if you are really good at what you do, your "thousand-aires" will become millionaires. So treat everyone like they are millionaires... unless you don't believe in yourself.

CHAPTER 7

THE VISION

I envision the creation of a modern-day "Model T Ford" idea by replacing the banks with an assembly line of equal opportunity lenders eager to serve you, your buyers and investors. Simply put, my vision is to become the Henry Ford of real estate. Just as Henry Ford created the first inexpensive, mass-produced automobile and revolutionized American industry, I envision revolutionizing the real estate business by going beyond just putting buyers and sellers together. What I envision is a real estate culture of doing business that also puts buyers and lenders together...all under one roof.

Let's face it: there will always be buyers, whether they want to live in the property, be a landlord and rent it out for income, or flip it. Everyone needs a roof over their head. But the absence of financing has shut the door on many people's dream of home ownership.

I proclaim a new dawn of investment that brings back pride of ownership!

This is a Main Street solution, not a Wall Street solution or a government solution. Living decently is a human right! To review what I described in Chapter 2, the concept is to put together real estate "dealerships" where everything can be done under one roof, much like car dealerships that are "sign and drive," but in the case of real estate dealerships, it is known as:

"Sign and Reside."

Ah....pride of ownership. Let's focus for a moment on how important this is. When a person rents a car, for example, in most cases they don't treat it the same way as if they owned it. For instance, you would not take your rental car to be detailed, or put expensive rims on the wheels, or spend on a body kit. Likewise with renting a property. Renters usually don't care if the lights are left on when the common areas are not in use, or if the hot tub is running with nobody in it, or if garbage is strewn about, or if the property is marked with graffiti. Having a society with no owners produces a society with no pride.

We need to bring back pride of ownership.

Pride of ownership comes because they own it. Ultimately, what people want is a good, clean, and affordable place to live. In my experience, I found that most buyers are already living in the neighborhood...they want to buy but don't know that they can.

Affordability is key. I advocate that buyers should

own the house, not let the house own them. The BHPH Real Estate System, with its flexibility and pool of un-limited equal opportunity lenders, can make housing truly affordable for one and all, once and for all!

Imagine wanting to buy a home but having no idea how to get it. It is as if the home were on an island, out of your reach. Your options are to either build a bridge to the island, or you can learn how to swim. BHPH Real Estate builds that bridge. The point is that you need to take a good look at where you are now, figure out where you want to be, and make a plan on how to get there.

I urge renters to consider buying even if they have bad credit. Lenders, buyers, and sellers need to all work together. Sure, the buyer will pay a premium, but it is worth it. Eventually, the mortgage will be paid off, but paying rent is forever. Waiting for the ideal time to buy a house is not the solution. That would be like waiting to drive until you have all green lights!

In BHPH Real Estate, both the buyer and seller are dependent on the lender, and their mutual cooperation is imperative to making a deal work. This new culture of doing business means that everyone needs to work together. In traditional real estate, if the buyer cannot get financing, then they cannot buy the property, which means the seller is forced to look for a new buyer, and the lender will not realize any profit on his money.

Traditional financing has become biased and is not an equal opportunity lender. It doesn't make sense that so many people have car payments for close to what they pay in rent, yet they could never imagine paying cash for a $30,000 car. When you go into a car dealership, you are bombarded with signs that may advertise that the vehicle is "only $250 per month" when in reality, you may be paying tens of thousands of dollars for that car. Yet you are able to sign a few papers, perhaps leave a small down payment, and within a matter of hours, you are on the road in your new car.

The same holds true for buying furniture. How often have you seen advertisements for "no down payment" and "no interest" until several years into the future? And the transaction is done with no hassle, all in-house. Why, you can even finance your college education... regardless of your credit and certainly not needing any employment.

But when it comes to real estate, there is no synergy between the parties. The current system is broken and does not work. I propose bringing everything together under one roof, making it hassle-free, convenient, easy, and most importantly, affordable. Therefore it's official:

Buy Here Pay Here Real Estate offers the first-ever real estate "dealership."

Some of its listings are the units that it owns as inventory, and the other listings are like traditional real estate. The idea is to take the concepts in this BHPH Real Estate book and apply them to your business practice whether you are a lender, an investor, real estate agent, broker or whatever your profession may be. Acquire an appreciation for and understanding of what financing adds. The uniqueness of BHPH Real Estate is that you have access to an arsenal of lenders whom you can speak with directly, all sitting at the same table where the deal is being put together...not fractionalized.

BHPH Real Estate cuts out the middleman and stream-lines the business. It makes doing business convenient. How you apply it is up to you.

Most real estate professionals are also real estate buyers. So isn't it natural for a real estate "dealership" to have its own inventory? And if their inventory is so good, shouldn't they also offer financing?

Let me share with you my vision and my dream for the BHPH Real Estate philosophy. Picture this:

A car filled with hard-working parents and their children is cruising down the road on a hot summer day with the windows rolled down and the radio playing softly in the background muffled only by the sound of intermittent gusts of wind and the soft giggles of children's laughter. They cherish their aimless drives together as it affords them a brief escape from their problems and lets them dream of a better life. A life free of worrying about working hard but only being able to barely pay the rent and bills. A life free from constantly being flooded with uncertainty about whether their children will be able to go to college, or if they will have anything left to leave them, or whether their children are destined to enter the same trap of only being able to just scrape by.

As they delve deeply into their thoughts, something grabs their attention. It could be a brightly colored billboard illuminated by the side of the road, or a radio commercial that has seeped into their subconscious.

81

Whatever it is, it awakens them from their worries and gives them direction. It is as if the words on the advertisement were written specifically for them. "Why Rent When You Can Own?" "Fire Your Landlord!" "One-Stop Shopping" and most enticing, "Sign and Reside" all beckon to them. The message carries the familiar sales practice of "Low-Down, Easy Monthly Payments" that actually helps them to afford many of their possessions, including the car they are driving, which makes this kind of weekend afternoon road trip possible..

Eager to seize the opportunity, they follow the advertisement's call to action and their aimless drive develops a new direction that will change their destiny.

They are directed to a former rental community where the clubhouse has been converted to an attractive sales office, while another unit has been transformed into a billiard room and Wi-Fi café. As they pull up to the free valet parking, they see brightly colored welcome flags perched high atop the property waving in the wind. Signs proclaiming "Low-Down, Easy Monthly Payments" and "One-Stop Shopping" evoke feelings of hope and confidence that this may be their dream come true.

As they step out of the car, they notice children playing in a safely staffed and secure play yard outfitted with the latest in outdoor equipment. There is a large, brightly polished barbecue grill cooking up a delectable aroma of freshly grilled hot dogs and crisp corn-on-the-cob, and a large case of cold sodas and water...all offered for free.

They can't help but delight in seeing their children join the other children, many with ketchup framing the smiles on their faces as they make new friends. The youngsters exude excitement at the prospect of growing up there. As the parents enter the clubhouse, they take a moment to look around. They see the billiard room, the Wi-Fi café, and then catch a glimpse of the shimmering blue clubhouse pool calling out to them on a hot summer day. They are warmly greeted by a friendly, no-pressure sales representative. She welcomes them to the community and offers them a cold drink, which they graciously accept. As they are sipping their icy sodas, she explains that she and her colleagues do not work off of commission, so it does not matter whether they buy the most expensive unit, or the least expensive unit. There is no benefit to her or anyone there to sell them something that they cannot afford — thus, no pressure.

Taking comfort in the sales representative's assurances, they begin to discuss their housing needs and what they are able to afford. After hearing them out, she says that she has three different models that would suit their needs perfectly. In addition, they may be able to pay the same, if not less, than they are currently paying in rent. They were obviously pleased to hear that.

Next, the sales representative offers to take them in a golf cart to show them the three prospective units as part of a tour around the community. Each of the units they see is clean and move-in ready. The units are completed in a neutral color scheme, all uniform and ready for them to add their own personal touches. Many of the appliances still have plastic on them, and all of the warranty papers, paint samples, and a list of subcontractor and vendor phone numbers are all conveniently located within the unit.

PROCESS FOR BUYERS

APPLICATION

LOW DOWN PAYMENT

BUYER SIGNS PAPERS AND TAKES RESPONSIBILITY OF THE UNIT (REPAIRS, ETC.)

BUYER IS ABLE TO MOVE INTO UNIT

LOW MONTHLY INTEREST PAYMENTS FOR SET PERIOD

CREDIT REPAIR IF NEEDED

OPTION TO PURCHASE OR REFINANCE THE UNIT ON OR BEFORE THE END OF SET PERIOD

After selecting the unit that would work best for them, they head back to the clubhouse where they fill out an application. Background checks and credit checks are completed within minutes and the sales representative comes back with good news. Although their credit was not good, which was no surprise to them, and no conventional lender would extend credit to them at this time, they are approved for in-house financing. All of the terms are explained to them in detail, including how much their down-payment will be, how much their monthly payment will be, and the fact that their interest rate will be higher than at a conventional bank, but it gives them the chance to get into a property today and start rebuilding their credit. It is explained that if they proceed with the deal, their payments will be due on the first of every month. Once they develop a history of paying on time, the credit bureaus will be notified of their timely payments, thus establishing good credit. She offers other suggestions to help improve their credit which will expedite a loan. She also introduces them to their preferred credit counseling agent who can continue working with them to strengthen their credit, and help facilitate obtaining a conventional loan.

Needless to say, words cannot describe their excitement. With the stroke of a pen, they are now on their way to realizing their dream of home ownership. The enthusiasm that one has when buying their first car is the only thing that can remotely compare to this feeling of excitement. Once all documentation is signed, their move-in date is set, and the keys are placed into their hands, along with cheers of congratulations.

Sign and reside...complete!

Simple. Convenient. One-stop shopping. That is the beauty and ease of the BHPH Real Estate System!

Now that you see how an ideal BHPH Real Estate transaction can be conducted, you will understand and see how this can be scaled down or scaled up. Whether it is a single-unit apartment, condo, house, townhouse, mansion, mobile home, vacant piece of property, or even a small city, the principles and the system remain the same.

CHAPTER 8

THE SYSTEM

Recently, I bumped into a very familiar person in the grocery store. It was the parent of one of my high school friends. I couldn't believe how long it had been since I last heard from the family. I went up to say hi, and we engaged in the customary back and forth banter: "What's your son been up to?" "How is the rest of the family?" After some additional benign chit-chat, the inevitable question came up, "What do you do?"

I proudly respond, "Real estate development and investing." Of course his reaction was not unexpected: he burst out laughing. Just because everyone else they know is doing badly in real estate, he figured that I was too. I was undaunted by his reaction because my philosophy is when times are good, I am good. But when times are bad, I am even better, as proven by my successful track record.

You see, in a down market, there is less competition, and those companies and investors that were unable to make it in the business, are now out of business.

I recently learned that one of my mortgage brokers, who infamously referred to himself as the "sub-prime king" and was known for giving out unsustainable loans, went back to school to get his degree in psychology or history or something. Meanwhile, I decided to work on reinventing and revolutionizing the real estate business as we know it, by putting into action the vision that I had: putting buyers and lenders together.

I started close to home. The buyers came from Craigslist and I was the lender. My average returns were between 25 percent and 30 percent, and that was just my cash-on-cash return, interest alone, not including the principle and my anticipated profit. The numbers were spectacular! But even with these great numbers, where did all the investors go?

I realized that what was natural and obvious to me wasn't to everyone else, and that is the purpose of this book...to teach my vision not as a dream, but to teach it as a practice and a reality.

So I set out investing in more and more of these little units. I am not going to sugar-coat it and say they were all turn-key units and in beautiful condition. The fact is that a lot of them were truly ugly ducklings. But I know how to turn an ugly duckling into a swan. After all, that was my full-time job: real estate investment. I soon owned a lot of units that generated income, but I realized that if I kept purchasing at the rate I was going, I would eventually run out of capital. So just being the lender was not enough; I needed recirculation of funds.

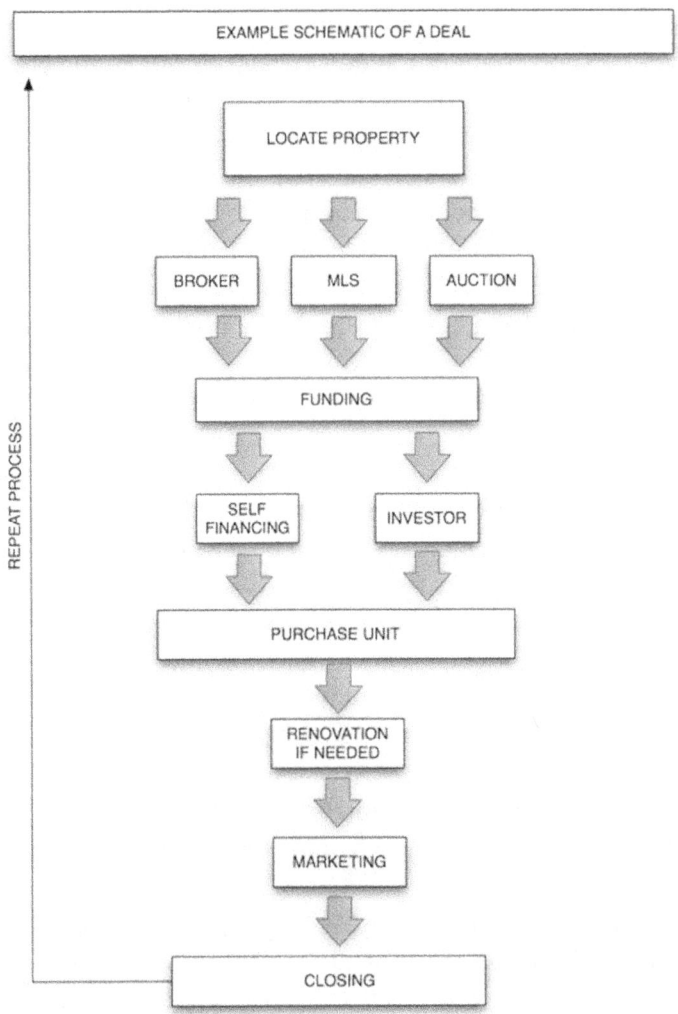

So whom did I go to? I went to investors. Not real estate investors, but investors who typically invest in stocks, bonds and mutual funds. Don't kid yourself, they too laughed at real estate, but I got the last laugh when I showed them the numbers. After all, in the end, that is what it is all about: the numbers. I was able to refinance all of my properties and pull out some of my profit ahead of the five-year balloon payment by tapping into hard-money loans at 12 percent. (A balloon mortgage is when the interest rate on a loan is fixed for a certain period of time, typically five to seven years. At the end of the specified time, the remaining balance on the mortgage becomes due. For example, if you had a $100,000 balloon mortgage and you paid off $15,000 in principle over five years, then at the end of that five-year period, the remaining balance of $85,000 would become due. Most people don't have the $85,000 balance to pay off their mortgage in full so they refinance the loan for the remaining balance. The advantage of a balloon mortgage is that it allows you to have lower monthly payments and typically lower interest rates.)

I did not care about paying the 12 percent in interest, because my return was 25 to 30 percent!

When given the opportunity to borrow someone else's money and still make a profit...go for it!

I still do not understand why people who have cash to buy a $100,000 home do so, so that they can say they own their home free and clear, instead of taking out a government FHA loan at 3 percent down (and depending on the interest rate, it is usually half of what I pay on a hard money loan). I find it to be smarter to either use the FHA loan, or what I call the "government gift" loan, because no one in their right mind would lend out that money for thirty years at that rate without government backing and subsidies — and take that extra cash... almost $97,000 and buy up a few units and "Buy Here Pay Here" them.

Of course I already see the arguments coming..."I am too busy to do this"..."I don't have the time." No problem. Instead of chasing deals, have people chasing you with deals.

Become a lender; become the leverage.

If a deal is good enough, the money will follow. Just hoping is not enough.

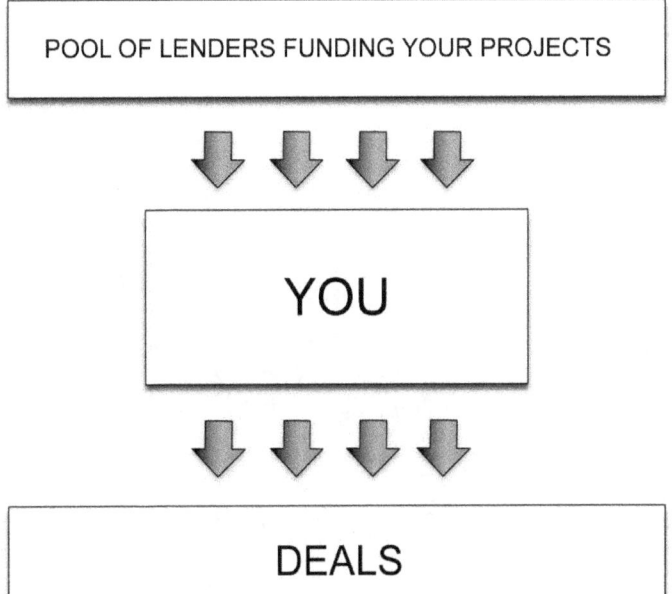

I like to work in circles. The first circle comprises your friends and family. Go to them for advice first and for money second. Then expand your circle to include associates. By using your network of family, friends, associates and acquaintances, the rings in your circle will develop into a way to raise money. Remember that no investment is too small...be an equal opportunity borrower, even if that means having to fund a $99,000 house with 99 people at $1,000 each.

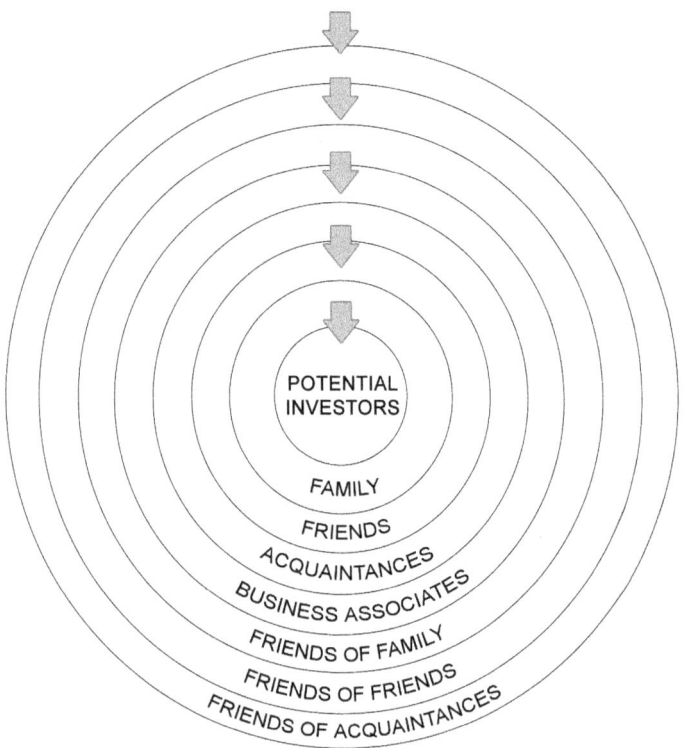

My first home purchase involved many different lenders and my latest one also includes many lenders, partners, etc., but at the end of the day, I got the deal funded. Interest rates do not really matter. If two or four points make a difference, then the margins are too tight. I suggest you walk away from the deal. I have two rules that I always follow:

Rule # 1: Don't lose money.

Rule # 2: Don't forget Rule #1.

The mechanics of the BHPH Real Estate System work as follows: If, for example, you purchase a $20,000 condominium...no secrets or tricks here...a straight purchase which can be found many ways such as on the MLS (multiple listing service), or at an estate sale, a foreclosure, or a tax auction, just to name a few. Trust me...these deals do exist and are out there. You just have to know where to look for them. Remember, as described in Chapter 6, you can often go to real estate offices and ask them to print out everything listed for sale on the MLS for under $25,000. If there are not a lot of units, bump up the request to everything under $50,000 and so on until you reach the point of saturation. You can also go to auctions and buy properties for pennies on the dollar (which anyone can do).

Then apply the following process: after finding the property and funding the purchase, whether through your own money or a lender's money, you do some light cosmetic cleanup (e.g., painting, cleaning or changing out the carpet, freshening up the bathrooms, replacing light fixtures, etc.). The key is that "neat and clean" sells.

Let's say worst-case scenario, you're into the unit for $25,000 including purchase, cleanup and some carrying costs. You then go ahead and list the unit for sale for $50,000 with $5,000 down, representing 10 percent of the new sales price. You take the $5,000 down payment and the remaining $45,000 balance you hold in creative financing. This can be executed in many ways, such as an option contract, often referred to as a contract for deed, or a lease purchase, or whatever you want to call it. Basically it means that you prefer to hold title to the property until the whole purchase price is paid in full and until then collect a fee that reflects an interest rate or "rent on your money" on not only the money you invested, but what profit you've created on paper. As always, I recommend that you consult an attorney regarding the applicable laws in your state.

You advertise the unit for sale: low-down, easy monthly payments. You accept $5,000 down, and monthly payments of only $800. These units typically rent in excess of $1,000 per month. The $800 includes the interest payment (which can also be referred to as an option fee) for the outstanding balance of $45,000, which consists of $450 per month, plus the Homeowners Association maintenance fees if any, taxes, insurance and reserve. (Always carry a reserve for unforeseen expenses.)

With this in mind, you still make an impressive 27 percent return, cash on cash.

One may ask how is it possible to make a 27 percent cash-on-cash return if you are only charging 12 percent? It's possible because the 12 percent is not only on the money you have out, which is $25,000 minus the $5,000 option fee (which is $20,000 at this point), but you are charging 12 percent on the profit that you created on paper. That is an additional $25,000 combined with the $20,000 you have out for the purchase, minus the $5,000 option fee, equals the $45,000 balance at 12 percent. That is: $450 per month x 12 months = $5,400 per year, divided by $20,000, which is the cash you have out of pocket, equals your 27 percent return.

I typically make the agreement for a five-year term. The buyer is further encouraged by not being charged a prepayment penalty, enabling them to pay us off or buy us out at any time. I don't care about the 12 percent; I am thrilled to double my money any day of the week...so we encourage them to get a conventional loan. A dollar in your pocket is better than two on the shelf.

**We never say no to a profit.
Take it and roll it into another deal.**

Taking it a step further, if the buyer takes the full five years to pay off the property (whether by refinancing it or paying the balance in cash) then the total payments paid over those five years would be $27,000 which represents the $450 a month being made in payments, multiplied by 12 monthly payments in the year for five years, which equals $27,000. When you then add the $25,000 profit being made on the sales price to the $27,000 being made on the payments, you make a total of $52,000 having only $20,000 out of pocket. This represents an incredible 260 percent return on your money over five years...which is a 52 percent return annually!

No matter how you slice it, the BHPH Real Estate System helps you maximize profits while reducing your property management and ultimately creating a deal that is affordable and achievable for most renters, if not any renter.

So your buyers are out there. Put them together with a lender and yourself as the investor and everyone will benefit. Even if you had to borrow the original $20,000 at 15 percent interest, you still are ultimately making 52 percent, not including the fact that the leverage would ultimately bring up your yield if you choose to fund it that way.

Now, I am not necessarily telling you to borrow money at 15 percent or that when you purchase a property you need to double the sales price to make it a good deal. These scenarios are only to serve as examples and are not typical. All deals and results may vary. Ultimately, when it comes to pricing, it must be priced affordably so that your potential buyers can afford it, thereby ensuring everyone's success.

This deal structure, which I have simulated using the BHPH Real Estate System, instills the value of pride of ownership in your buyer.

You set a predetermined sales price for the property, and any maintenance issues now become their issues. All of the terms are written up in a triple net lease (where the tenant is responsible to pay for all of the maintenance and expenses) and if they do not pay their monthly payments, then the BHPH Real Estate rule kicks in: "You don't pay...you don't stay." For a few hundred dollars, you can hire an eviction attorney, which I highly recommend you have on your team, and let them handle all of the eviction work. Then turn around and repeat the process again and again, taking another $5,000 down and selling the unit. We hope to have the need to only sell it once, but if we are struck by what seems to be the misfortune of turnover, which in any other business system would be your downside, in our case this is your upside. If you receive $5,000 from five people, you practically have the unit for free.

A common question is: Why don't these people buy these units themselves? Because more people have $5,000 than $25,000...it's that simple. What if they don't have the $5,000 down payment? Ultimately, you decide what the minimum will be to let them move in.

There have been times that I let people move in with $4,000 down and split the $1,000 balance owed over the next couple of months, keeping in mind that if they miss one payment, they are out. I know it sounds harsh, but you have to run your business like a business and train your tenants and the people who do business with you. Because if they think they can get away with it, they will continue to try getting away with it again and again. It's human nature. If by the third day they are late, or whatever your lease governs, a notice goes upon their door, and the eviction process begins. It is the hefty up-front payment that keeps them vested in the property.

And here we come full circle to the importance of being an eternal learner.

Most people don't take their learning beyond the school gates, but in actuality, it is outside of the gates when the work really begins...trying to make money, pay bills, find investments, etc. We want to help people keep themselves out of the trap. But how? Financial education is the answer. It is important to be an *"eternal learner."* I have read lots of books, bought and sold tons of properties, and looked at endless opportunities out there.

> **I believe that if you cannot get a job making what you want to earn, then get a job doing what you want to learn.**

It's okay to eat humble pie once in a while, and sometimes it is necessary.

When the real estate market crashed and it seemed as if my business was going to fall apart, I reinvented myself and revolutionized real estate in the process. It's the concept of not only being the lender, buyer or investor, but also being the lender in any one of those situations. For example. BHPH Real Estate puts a lender in place like a car dealership: even if the dealership doesn't offer financing in-house, they sure will help you find a loan.

I invented a system that uses the flipper and landlord hand-in-hand: the landlord brings in income and the flipper brings in the capital gains. But the BHPH Real Estate System puts it all under one transaction, one contract, one roof, so to speak.

The synergy between the lenders, buyers and investors is crucial, as displayed on the illustartion on the next page. The connection between the lender and the buyer ultimately creates the underlying profit for the foundation of that triangle, which is the investor. The triangle is an isosceles triangle, making it equal for participants on all sides.

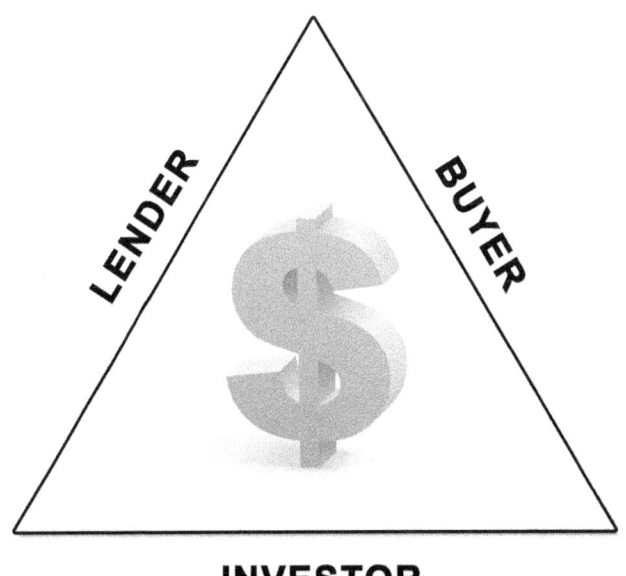

INVESTOR

It should be a win-win-win for all, with everyone benefiting from the deal: from the buyer who is able to get a new lease on life and get into a property, to the lender who makes a higher return than they would ever be able to make in the bank, and the investor who makes his money by ultimately consummating the deal between the lender and the buyer.

Ultimately, the BHPH Real Estate System is one from which everyone can benefit. And should.

We don't need a financial system where Wall Street wins and Main Street loses. We need a system in which everyone wins. And this way, no one will ever need to Occupy Wall Street again.

CHAPTER 9

JOIN THE REVOLUTION!

Buy Here Pay Here Real Estate is a real-life application of the *art of money making money* from which anyone can profit and benefit once they commit to being a lender, buyer or investor. The most common question I am asked is: "How can I get involved?"

The beauty of this system is that it creates abundance for all and does not discriminate. Not everyone will participate in the system in the same ways I have (as a lender, buyer, and investor). Each of us is unique, and wouldn't it be incredibly boring if we were all carbon copies of one another? In any economy, some people are lenders, some are buyers and some are investors. It's when there is a disproportionate amount of financing that the real estate system, which is a huge part of our economy, screeches to a halt.

The first way to join this revolution is to adopt a "Buy Here Pay Here" perspective when looking at your own financial situation. On an individual level, this involves determining where you are and where you want to be *wealthwise.* Set realistic goals for yourself. One of the reasons why I like real estate is because you would never be homeless (like I mentioned earlier, if a deal goes bad, you can at least pop a tent and live on the property until you get up and running again). By considering what funds you have available to you, you can decide whether you want to be a buyer. If you don't like driving around looking at real estate, this may not be the business for you. You might opt to be a lender instead.

If you do decide to become a buyer, I suggest that you save money and don't buy a house beyond your means. I don't even recommend buying necessarily. Some areas simply do not make sense...sounds crazy from a real estate guy, but it's true. Why buy an $800,000 condo when you can rent the same unit for $3,500 per month, like in New York City? Sometimes it is best to rent and save the additional money to invest it in real estate whether as a buyer, lender or investor, who uses the BHPH Real Estate System. If you are able to go to an area that has affordable housing (according to my definition of affordable housing, of course) I urge you to. The days of "big hat, no cattle" and "looking good but going nowhere" are over. There is a ton of land out there and an abundance of housing if you chose to seize the opportunities.

When looking for a property, whether to rent or buy, I encourage you to work with someone who is of the Buy Here Pay Here culture and understands these philosophies and ideas: the need to keep properties affordable, the need for convenience, and the benefits of a one-stop shop.

After reading this book, if you realize that you too want to get in on the action, then welcome to the club!

We are glad to have you on board. A revolution always needs more like-minded people. You can do it too, whether you are a lender, buyer, or investor.

By the way, flip is my favorite 4-letter "f" word and has made me tons of money. But that is because I have not only flipped, but also flopped...and learned. It is important that when you buy a property to flip, you should know what you are doing first. Education is key. This book and many other online resources will help you with the tools necessary to make educated decisions. With the education in hand, your first goal should be to go out and buy properties where you add value, whether physical or financial value, and then flip it for a profit.

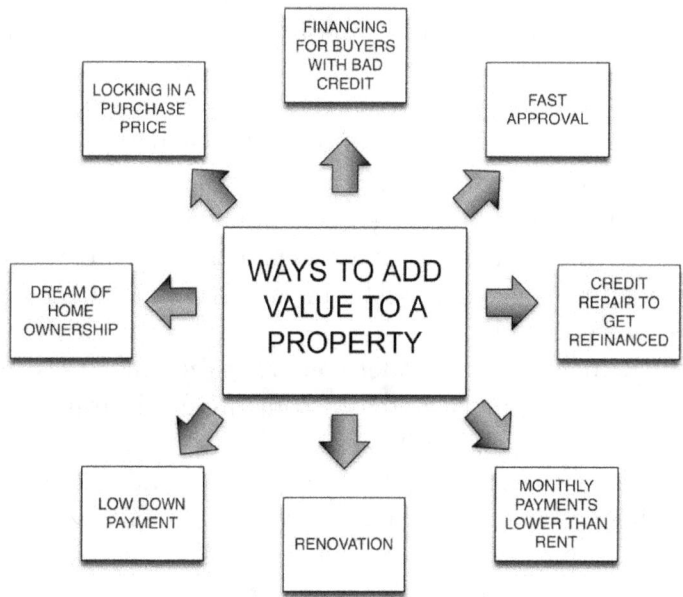

Another option is to be a landlord, where you can rent out the property for the income to at least cover the expenses. After all, landlords do a good job of providing good affordable temporary housing (it is considered temporary because lifelong tenants are few and far between; the average tenant usually last about three years). So being in the landlord business, you have to understand your full-time job becomes a management position, and in larger projects especially, it is a full-time job managing the managers. You'll want to be sure that you understand what you are getting into first. After reading this book, at least you see that you can create the same rental income and reap the appreciation and taxable depreciation while paying long-term capital gains without all the landlord-management headaches.

As a buyer, whether flipping or being a landlord, find good counsel and like-minded people who understand what your end goal is. If you are in debt, make your first goal to get out of debt. If drowning, first get your head above water. If you have excess cash, but work too hard at a 9-to-5 job and can't be in the business of real estate, then I say invest in real estate. With money in your pocket, deals will find you. It is your job to know what a good deal is.

Remember, as a lender you are in the catbird's seat. Only lend to people who have something to lose and are vested in the deal. If it is so good, let people put their money where their mouth is. I suggest people with extra cash lend, buyers buy, and investors put deals together for both parties. Continue educating yourself, realizing that it is impossible for you to know everything and so when need be, rent the knowledge. You can rent the knowledge from the best accountant in the country for $500 an hour. He is letting you borrow his thirty years of experience. The same holds true for other professionals like painters, plumbers and handymen. If you know you can't do everything, then quit while you are ahead and hire a professional to get the job done right.

You join the BHPH Real Estate revolution by participating and applying these formulas and my formulas in your everyday life, whether you are looking to buy a property and have little money to put down...or if you own your house outright, have cash in the bank, and money in stocks, you are needed, too. If you don't like the idea of being a lender, guess what? You already are! Most people don't realize this: if you have money in the bank, the bank then uses your money to lend to everyone else but you, and at a higher interest rate than what they are willing to lend it to you for, if at all. So essentially, the banks are flipping your money! Remember, you can either use leverage (borrow) or be leveraged (lend). Doing nothing nowadays is not an option.

If you are making less than 5 percent on your money, you are losing between inflation and lost opportunities.

If you're not in the market or inclined to buy, then you join the revolution by becoming a lender. If you have no money, then start building equity. If you have money, then become an empowered lender. And I just shared the reasons as to why you are a lender already. If knowing this is not enough to be comfortable, I believe in lending in teams or groups, such as private place-ment funds. In such funds, the decisions on where the money goes per deal is decided on a local and intimate level, returns are much higher, and risks are spread out over more people. These groups are able to achieve this because their strength is in numbers. By becoming in-volved in such groups, you are able to and can afford to hire better professionals and counsel, plus you spread the workload and risk out over many different people. My philosophy is that when starting out in real estate, everyone is all better off thinking: "If I am the smart-est person at the table, we are all in trouble." Surround yourself with smart, trustworthy people. And remember, you do not need to acquire knowledge that is rentable.

I have personally been involved in lending in pri-vate placement funds, which typically employ full-time fund managers and a compliance officer, and have the best professionals on retainer. And ever since I joined in these groups, deals now come to me; I don't have to go to them. When you have money, deals somehow find you, like bees to honey. If you want to be a buyer and you need the money, your job then is to educate people on the BHPH Real Estate System and how it can work for them. Explain to someone who does not want to get his or her hands dirty as a buyer (which you, like I was, may be more than willing to do) the benefit of becom-ing a lender. It is a misconception that the only way to invest in real estate is to either live in it, rent it or flip it—because you can find hard workers willing to do the dirty work. You might want to even consider starting an angel investment group yourself.

Having read this book, you will now be able to spot like-minded people. If they are not like-minded, get them on the same page. It will benefit everybody: lenders, buyers, investors, and the overall economy.

Timing is important, as is recognizing when you are at the right place at the right time. Successful people know when to seize an opportunity and how to capitalize on it. For example, the human population is growing exponentially. This means that the demand for more affordable housing will inevitably rise significantly over the years. In bad economies, many people prefer to rent rather than buy. Because rents tend to go up with inflation, owning rental properties can be very lucrative. BHPH Real Estate shows you not only how to strategically position yourself for success in any economy, but also how important pride of ownership is. This is not something I was taught in school; rather, it is what I discovered through real-world observation and experience.

The Buy Here Pay Here Revolution is the idea of not being passive waiting for banks.

It's the idea that *you* can replace the banks and *you* are your largest investor. Until recently, all but a select few have been waiting for the government or bank or some large governing body to tell us it's OK. Well, I am telling you it is OK. Whether it's $150,000 or $15,000, our dollar is not going down in value...on the contrary! Your buying power increases tenfold if you choose to pursue these opportunities available to you.

The BHPH Real Estate System blends creative financing with brilliant innovations governed by professionals. After all, you can't charge just any interest rate and there are laws in the United States especially when it comes to real estate lending and investing. After completing many hundreds of transactions, I have boiled this down to not just an art, but a science.

And this is just the beginning. There is more to know and to learn. There are only so many pages one book can hold. I encourage you to follow me on my blog at www.LarryBieda.com, where you can find valuable updates, supplements and additional resources about the BHPH Real Estate System.

THEOPPORTUNITYISNOWHERE

Reading the above heading, what do you see? If you are a pessimist, you read it as THE OPPORTUNITY IS NOWHERE. However, if you are an optimist, you read it as THE OPPORTUNITY IS NOW HERE! So which one is right? They both are, so whatever you believe is true for you. You must train your mind to filter out the negativity. Understand that if you are broke now, it is only temporary, but poor is eternal. I know a lot of football and basketball players, among other high net-worth people, who made their money but know nothing about money and how to keep it, grow it and protect it.

I congratulate you on taking this first step along this road and I look forward to being with you along your journey to success!

Sincerely,

Larry L. Bieda
Author of *Buy Here Pay Here Real Estate* and
Founder of the Buy Here Pay Here Real Estate System

ACKNOWLEDGMENTS

This book is a testimony to all the people who have always believed in me and pushed me to keep moving forward. So many special people encouraged me and taught me that making money was only half the fun, but teaching others to do the same is not only a possibility, but a responsibility.

I would like to acknowledge the following people that if not for them, this book would not be possible and the question "why can't we do it this way?" would have quite possibly never left my mind so this book could flourish into what it is today.

These people believed in me and the idea that housing and wealth weren't reserved for the elite few. They saw Buy Here Pay Here Real Estate truly as an IPO (initial public offering) with tons of potential and they graciously gave of their time and talents to make this a reality.

A special thanks to Penelope Love, who helped me find "my writer's voice": you are a talented, kind and gentle person whom I have enjoyed working with.

To Frank McKinney: thanks for your blessing and encouragement. You are not only my inspiration but my aspiration.

To Stephen Muss, who always believed in me and my family and treated us like part of his family: thank you for setting such demanding work ethics and high standards and teaching us how to achieve them. We are truly grateful for your always helping us even when we called you out of the "bleau"!

To Robert Daniels: thank you for believing in me and my family and giving us our first leg up. You gave us a hand up, not a hand out, a loan and not a gift, and for that we are eternally grateful.

To Dave P: I will keep my commitment to continue paying it forward and passing it on. Thank you for your sage advice.

To Sonny Kahn: thank you for sending me and my brother to sleep-away camp. I never forgot how nice a real estate developer could be and it gave me something to aspire to. You treated us to a summer of fun and allowed us kids to be kids, which was invaluable to us.

To Dr. Andy and Dr. David: thank you both for everything. Words cannot thank you enough for all that you have done.

To my loving family: I thank you for always trusting my judgment even when it seemed counter-intuitive or just outright crazy.

To my mother: thank you for always teaching me to keep fighting until hell freezes over and then to get up and fight on the ice! You are truly an inspiration to me. You told me to take the Bieda family name, shine it and make it something to be proud of so that it will illuminate the way for future generations. You taught me that the reason for the hard times we went through in our life was compared to the extreme heat that it takes in the smelting process to refine gold so that it ultimately reaches its highest and purest form.

Finally, to all those who are dear to me that are living or who have passed on and are watching from above. There are not enough words, paper, or ink to thank you enough for your guidance, love and support.

When I look at my life's journey, I envision footprints in the sand etched along the shore of a beautiful beach. Along the way, I see two sets of footprints. However, during the toughest times in my life, I only see one set. At first, one may think that during the hardest times I was alone and those were my lone footprints in the sand. But on the contrary, the other set of footprints were my mother's, my family, my friends, supporters, and of course G-d carrying me through the most difficult times of my life.

My thanks to all of you for always being there to lift me up when I am down and encourage me to soar as high as I want to, not because the sky is the limit, but because there is no limit to our potential. The only limits that we have are the ones we place on ourselves. Believe it and you can achieve it.

Remember: The opportunity is now here!

ABOUT THE AUTHOR

Larry L. Bieda is a successful entrepreneur, self-made millionaire, financial prodigy, speaker, consultant, coach, and real estate deal expert who has helped countless people throughout the United States and abroad with his proven strategies to achieve financial success. As the author of *Buy Here Pay Here Real Estate*, and founder and creator of the Buy Here Pay Here Real Estate System, Larry is widely admired for his keen eye in recognizing the hidden potential and seeing value in distressed properties. His philosophy is that everyone should have the ability to achieve the American Dream of home ownership and be able to buy good quality affordable homes. His method offers both buyers and investors creative programs that feature a convenient one-stop shopping approach, which covers every aspect of the home-buying and investment experience.

Learn more about Larry's thoughts on his personal blog at www.LarryBieda.com.